Growing Up Jewish

THE SEARCH FOR IDENTITY

Helen Wolfers

Melbourne Australia

Copyright © 2020 by Helen Wolfers.

All rights reserved. No part of this publication may be reproduced, distributed or transmitted in any form or by any means, including photocopying, recording, or other electronic or mechanical methods, without the prior written permission of the publisher, except in the case of brief quotations embodied in critical reviews and certain other non-commercial uses permitted by copyright law. For permission requests, write to the publisher, addressed "Attention: Permissions Coordinator," at the address below.

Helen Wolfers c/- Intertype
Unit 45, 125 Highbury Road
BURWOOD VIC 3125
www.intertype.com.au

Self-publishing support services by www.intertype.com.au

Ordering Information:
Quantity sales. Special discounts are available on quantity purchases by corporations, associations and others. For details, contact the "Special Sales Department" at the address above.

Growing Up Jewish in Australia - Helen Wolfers
ISBN 978-0-6487977-8-4

First and foremost I would like to thank Nicolas Brasch, festival director of the Melbourne Jewish Book Week, who read an earlier iteration of this book and wholeheartedly rejected it on every possible level. When I had recovered from the shock, I realized that he was absolutely correct and did a complete re-write. To quote William Blake –

"Damn braces - bless relaxes".

I then requisitioned the services of my close friend and literary editor, Aviva Layton in Los Angeles , to whom I am most grateful for her generous help in the onerous task of re-editing this book.

When I was very tiny my parents would ask me in Yiddish

"Wus bist du?" (What are you?)

and I would reply to their delight:

"A Yiddisher Maydele" ("A little Jewish girl")

Contents

INTRODUCTION 5

IN THE BEGINNING 15

AUTO DA FE' 25

SHYLOCK'S DAUGHTER 49

THE EXTINGUISHED SPARK 62

WHAT'S IN A FORESKIN? 78

ANTONIO'S SON 89

A MOUTHFUL OF WORMS 99

YERIDA* (The Descent) 133

THE WILDERNESS YEARS 145

JUDAISM TRANSCENDED 151

TO LONDON VIA HELL 162

A CHILLING SILENCE 171

AMERICA IS DIFFERENT 192

THE SECOND COMING 211

WHOSE MESSIAH? WHOSE JERUSALEM? 237

WHOSE TEMPLE, WHOSE HOLOCAUST? 253

WUS BIST DU? (What Are You?) 265

Introduction

In Rome today, in the ruins of the ancient Roman forum, tourists still flock to visit the Arch of Titus erected by the Romans to commemorate their victory over the Jews in Palestine two thousand years ago. By the fourth century of the common era there were thirty-six such memorial arches, each one commemorating a Roman victory over a nation of the ancient world.

So why, one may wonder, of all those conquered thirty-six nations are the Jews the only one still here today, and still practicing the same religion and speaking the same language as the Hebrew slaves depicted on the arch of Titus being led into Rome two thousand years ago.

In a short essay titled "Concerning the Jews" published in 1899, the famous American author Mark Twain asked the same question:

"…The Egyptian, the Babylonian, and the Persian rose, filled the planet with sound and splendour, then faded to dream-stuff and passed away; the Greek and the Roman followed, and made a vast noise, and they are gone; other peoples have sprung up and held their torch high for a time, but it burned out, and they sit in twilight now, or have vanished. The Jew saw them all, beat them all, and is now what he always was, exhibiting no decadence, no infirmities of age, no weakening of his parts, no slowing of his energies, no dulling of his alert and aggressive mind. *All things are mortal, but the Jew; all other forces pass but he remains.* What is the secret of his immortality?"

According to the Hebrew Bible when Moses asked the Jewish God what He was, He replied: "I am that I am" and Jewish sages have been debating what that means ever since.

Unlike all other gods of Biblical times such as Ra, the Egyptian sun god, or Baal the Canaanite god of war, the Hebrew God had neither name nor specificity of purpose: He is a god of everything and of nothing. This enigmatic open-endedness, this blank canvas, has forced each generation to define for itself what it means to be Jewish to best suit its own needs in its own time. And perhaps this is the reason for their immortality.

From ancient times up until the beginning of Jewish Emancipation at the end of the 18th century, Jews were unambiguously regarded as a people defined by their religion, both by themselves and everyone else.

Today Jews are still thought by many people, including many among themselves, to be both a religion and a people. But according to the World-wide Independent Network (WIN) survey on religion, carried out in 2012 in fifty-seven countries, Jews were found to be the least religious of all the major religions in the world today. Furthermore, they were the only category in which the majority described themselves as secular.

A "people" is defined by the Oxford dictionary as a large group of humans who share common racial and cultural traits. But today there are Jews of practically every conceivable racial and cultural background.

Apart from Ashkenazi and Sephardi Jews there are Chinese, Indian, Japanese, black American and Ethiopian Jews.

So, if Jews are no longer identifiable as a religion or a people, what makes them "Jewish"?

Sigmund Freud, the father of psychoanalysis was himself challenged by this question. Born into an assimilated German speaking Jewish family in 1856, Freud was first forced to confront his own Jewish identity when his theory of psychoanalysis was rejected and denigrated as a "Jewish science" by his anti-Semitic colleagues. Consequently he was constrained in his early years to lecture only to Jewish audiences. Here, to his surprise, he discovered a shared commonality with other Jews of which he had hitherto been unaware. In a letter to *Bnei Brit* (a Jewish social organisation) in Vienna in 1926, Freud wrote:

"There were other considerations (apart from anti-Semitism) which made the attractiveness of Judaism irresistible to me".

He went on to say that he had come to realise that there was something at the very core of him which was Jewish, which he could not yet identify, but which he was sure would one day be explained.

When I entered Sydney Girls High School in 1945 one of the questions on my enrolment form asked for my "racial identity". Not knowing which box to tick I asked the teacher and I was told that I was Caucasian. So I ticked Caucasian, even though I had never heard the word before and that night I looked it up in the Oxford dictionary and found that it meant "white skinned and of European origin". I had no problem with the white skin part but my parents, whose ancestors had lived in Poland for several centuries, had never considered themselves to be Poles or "of European origin". Ever since their expulsion from the land of Israel 2000 years ago Jews had always identified themselves as Jews and so had everybody else.

Before the modern era Jews had no problem retaining their Jewish identity: the rest of the world did it for them, often against their will. In the xenophobic, white, Anglo-Saxon Australia of my childhood foreigners were called "reffos", (and more often than not "bloody reffos"). All foreigners were mistrusted and none more than the Jews.

However, the realisation during the Second World War that Australia was too under-populated to defend itself gave rise to the postwar catch-cry: "Populate or Perish". In a concerted effort to increase the population the Australian government instigated the "Ten Pound Pom program in 1945 offering British migrants transport for £10 from England to Australia. The "reffos"of my childhood were renamed "New Australians" and migrants from most European countries, including some that had collaborated with the Nazis, were welcomed to Australia, but not the Jews.

A secret government white paper written at that time (but only released 30 years later) stated:

"A strict quota for Jews who had survived the war in Europe and Shanghai was imposed because of the negative effect that Jewish migration might have on

(Australia's new) immigration policy." Furthermore, the definition of "Jew" was based on racial not religious grounds. A Jewish member of the team responsible for the selection of eligible Jewish immigrants commented at the time: "Hitler could not have done better himself." (Susan Rutland: The Transformation of a Community).

In 1973 the White Australia policy was abolished, opening the doors to Asian immigration. By the turn of the century, with the instigation of yet another surge in the rate of immigration, the "New Australians" became "Australians of different ethnic back grounds" and we are now "Australians all".

Today more than half the citizens of Australia were not born in Australia or have at least one parent who was not born in this country. Minority groups are no longer discriminated against and Jews are now fully accepted as part of the Australian nation. To retain their Jewish identity the challenge for them now is to preserve their Jewishness in an increasingly secular open society with the intermarriage rate approaching fifty percent.

Due to the accelerating rate of intermarriage in all first world countries "who is a Jew" is becoming more and more difficult to define. Almost fifteen million people in the world now identify themselves as Jews. A further 17.8 million claim to be partly Jewish because one parent is Jewish. The Israeli "Law of Return" was amended in 1970 to include people who have at least one Jewish grandparent, or are married to a Jew, making 23.5 million people eligible to immigrate to Israel because of their Jewish identification.

The overwhelming majority of people identifying themselves as Jews outside of Israel live in the United States. A Pew survey designed to investigate Jewish identity in the U.S. found that "observing religious law is not relevant to most American Jews. Jewish identity is becoming increasingly more defined by culture and ancestry rather than religion (Pew Research Centre report 2013).Today for the majority of those identifying themselves as Jews, "who is a Jew" is anyone who says they are Jewish and "what is Jewish" is increasingly what one decides for oneself.

But all those identifying themselves as Jews automatically inherit the mythology and national history of the Jews as recorded in the Hebrew Bible.

In the Hebrew Bible it is written that God said to the Hebrew nation:

I have set you apart from all the other nations of the world (Leviticus 20:26)

The tension generated in navigating this difficult destiny in the modern world, to be simultaneously a "**part of**" and "**apart from**" all the other nations of the world, underpins much of the saga of growing up Jewish described in this book.

CHAPTER 1:

IN THE BEGINNING

When my parents immigrated to Australia from Poland in 1926. they did not come with any notion of becoming Australians. The concept of belonging to any country was unknown to them. Neither they nor the Poles had ever regarded them as Poles. They always saw themselves, as everyone else saw them, as Jews.

Jews were not persecuted in Australia and this was all my parents had really hoped for in their newly adopted homeland. But they were nevertheless still subjected to social and economic discrimination and to overcome these handicaps they hid their Jewishness. I clearly remember the unspoken secret in our house that my mother presented herself as a French Christian woman in her business connections and Mrs. Gland, a close Jewish friend in those early days, was some other sort of "Christian" outside the intimacy of our homes. For us children with broad Australian accents, there was no problem passing ourselves off as Christians or Jews when and as we pleased.

By the time of my appearance in 1932, my parents had achieved a small degree of lower middle-class comfort which to them and consequently to me, appeared undreamt of wealth. We had a car and a telephone, by no means universal commodities among middle-class Australians in the thirties. Food was cheap and plentiful and I grew up believing that the prime responsibility of every child - at least of every Jewish child - was to eat up well for the satisfaction of his or her parents.

There were secondary responsibilities too, like doing well at school, which would inevitably ensure one, at the very least, security and prosperity , and maybe even immortality as the next Freud or Einstein; or diligent practice on the violin, which might produce another Heifetz or Menuhin. We were injected with the accumulated frustrated ambitions of our parents' long sojourns in the ghettos of Europe.

To these I added an aspiration of my own: to be like other kids. Not the other children of my parents' tight supportive community, but the blond, blue-eyed Anglo-Saxon Australian kids I played with in the streets and at school. .

I cannot remember a single clearly anti-Semitic incident from my early childhood, but there is much circumstantial evidence and the more I dig now, the more I find. For example, I remember how, almost like a reflex, we children used to hush our parents when their voices rose in Yiddish in the streets and that they would not oppose us or reason with us, but docilely comply with our demand.

But there was one obstacle to "being like the other kids" which I could not overcome. Every Wednesday morning at school at 10 am. (remarkable how the day and time have imprinted themselves forever in my mind) while all the other Christian kids were meeting for their weekly hour of religious instruction in the main school assembly Hall, we twenty odd Jewish children were diverted to the form IV classroom where for five solid years, Mr. Rothfield, of blessed memory, succeeded in teaching us not one single recallable lesson on Judaism. From amongst the inmates of that class-room would emerge some of the state's top students in mathematics and history, geography and German, but not one of us could have passed a primary school exam in Bible Studies.

My parents and their friends brought with them from Poland an allegiance to Bundism, the socialist Yiddish movement of Eastern Europe. They were non or anti-religious, in revolt against centuries of mediaeval religiosity. The socialist bit died easily in the face of an open capitalist society, but they clung ferociously to *Yiddishkeit* (Jewishness), their true heritage, which they rightly feared would disappear if not perpetuated in us. Their hopes however were doomed from the outset. Yiddish was to us a renegade language. It represented the ghetto and all that set us apart, a barrier to the outside world with which we now had to merge. Although Yiddish was the language spoken at home most of us first generation Australian Jews grew up understanding but not speaking it. This was really quite a feat. A baby learns its first words from its parents, yet there was never any intermediate stage where we used Yiddish. Our parents spoke to us and to each other in Yiddish, but we answered only in English. We were renouncing our parents' Yiddishkeit as they were renouncing their parents' religiosity. We felt ashamed of it. We joined the ranks of millions of anti-Semites and European enlightened Jews to degrade it and all it represented.

Nevertheless, its soul survived. My earliest memories always include the sound of the elders speaking Yiddish; the infinite comfort and security of the soft murmurs of *"mamaloshen"* (mother tongue) issuing from the adjoining room when my light was switched off at night for sleep; of my father soothing me with a Yiddish lullaby that no doubt his mother sang to him, and, above all, the incomparable joys of Yiddish humour. It is to our credit that we were able to recognize and admit our appreciation of at least this small emotional core of our heritage, even before Black became beautiful and the Yiddish writer Isaac Bashevis Singer won a Nobel Prize for literature.

I developed a deep psychological chasm between the inside of my home and the outside world. My home became a place apart, a fortress of safety, warmth, and protection against the outside hostile world. And within the fortress there were two further buttresses against the menacing outside world: the *"boidem"* and the *"kaila"* (the attic and the cellar). The manhole to the *"boidem"* was inconveniently located over the bath in the bathroom, so that it could only be accessed by placing a specially constructed wooden straddle across the bath to support a ladder long enough to reach the ceiling above. Furthermore, these two pieces of equipment were kept in the *"kaila"*, presumably so that no intruder would be able to put the puzzle together and access the *"boidem"*. This elaborate strategy was designed to protect the *"sroira"* (merchandise), the naperies and draperies of my mother's interior decorating business which were stored in the *"boidem"*.

The *"kaila"* underneath the house was stuffed with history: a mountain of straw hats, a painful reminder of my father's failed business in the new country: non-perishable foods, enough to stock a grocery in case the war, then raging to our north were to invade us too. And somewhere buried in the bare soil under all this paraphernalia was a stash of money in a secret spot known only to my parents and me, the purpose of which was never actually explained to me. I assumed that if anything ever happened to my parents, I was to dig it up and somehow save myself, but exactly how I had no idea.

Coming as they had from a life of cruel hardship and violence where sudden death was not an infrequent possibility, my parents sought to protect me in their new environment as their parents had protected them by building a wall of defence against the Gentile world outside. Similarly, they thought they could protect me from the horrors at that time afflicting the Jews in Europe by simply hiding them from me. Consequently, I imbibed a confused and chaotic image of the world and our place in it. My parents transmitted to me a paradoxical image of the Europe in which they had grown up as both a heaven and a hell. All those horrors that they were whispering about around our dining room table were happening "over there" but all that was civilized and cultured was also "over there". Australia, was by contrast, a cultural wilderness to them.

I was about ten years old when the first reports of the Holocaust started filtering through to Australia. My parents sat around their dining room tables with their friends whispering in low voices. To protect us, our parents excluded us from whatever horrors they themselves were aware of. They would simply switch from Yiddish to Polish, which none of us children understood. This so annoyed me that in anger I coined a derogatory but onomatopoeic term for the Polish language: *"ooshchi-mooshchi"*.

"Stop talking *"ooshchi-mooshchi"*! I would yell in fury.

I don't know when I actually caught onto what they were whispering about, but I certainly knew that our cousins in Europe were in terrible danger. I also knew what they looked like from photographs, I knew their names and how old they were. I knew who their parents were and what they looked like. I sensed that the most macabre and murkiest of horrors were happening to them. Their Europe, my parents' Europe, became some eerie moonscape and the Warsaw Ghetto grew as a concept, rather than a place in my mind. I never spoke about it to anyone and never asked questions. This was the silent war I grew up with inside our home.

But outside there was another war going on, a bright exciting war, one we spoke of freely and questioned endlessly. There were searchlights over Sydney Harbor and Movietone News films in the cinemas, regular radio news updates, daily newspaper reports, wax instead of silver wrappers on our chewing gum, handsome Americans courting big sisters, fiery Churchillian speeches on the radio, wartime songs and wartime fashions. Sometimes on film, we saw people die in air raids and soldiers in battle, but somehow even this seemed part of a clean, daylight, speakable war.

But in that other war, the war inside my dining room, there were fleeting images of cattle trucks, of children torn from parents, wives from husbands, of suicides, slow starvation, instant ovens and smoking chimneys; of mud and murk as unimaginable and unspeakable as the interior of one's own grave. This was the Jewish war, being kept in custody inside our home along with the Yiddish and the *sroira* hidden up in the attic and the money buried down in the cellar.

I was six years old when the war began and eleven when it ended. During the time that I had completed my primary schooling, a million and a half Jewish children had been murdered in Europe. But for me Anti-Semitism was still a meaningless word and whatever it was that the adults were whispering about was happening "over there" in faraway Europe, on the other side of the planet.

CHAPTER 2

AUTO DA FE'

By the time I was born seven years after their arrival in Australia, my parents had graduated economically from selling shoelaces and shoe polish in their small stall in Paddy's Market to an itinerant soft-furnishing business.

In those days the wheat and sheep farmers were the wealthiest sector of society. These pioneering farmers were called "squatters" having taken possession of their land by simply squatting on it. Now, as the wealthiest class they became known as the squattocracy.

My parents travelled enormous distances to their homes to sell them my mother's versions of the latest European décor. Neither buyer nor seller had the faintest conception of what this was and my mother succeeded in actually creating the prevailing styles of interior decoration for the Australian "squattocracy" up till the mid-fifties when the outside world finally broke through the barriers of Australia's isolation. Her success grew and grew as Australia's leading families, the Baillieus, Myers and Darlings, families that have left their names on national corporations, monuments, mountains and rivers, vied for her latest creations in curtains and cushions.

Because my parents spent so much time travelling to sheep stations, I was launched on my career at boarding schools. At the age of four, I was sent to what must have been Australia's first alternative "open" school in 1936. The school, St, John's, was prosecuted several times for offending the public decency, as we swam and played in the nude on Parsley Bay, the beach across the road. There must have been some "back to nature" philosophy determining its principles. I remember very little of my time there, except that I was acutely miserable on Sunday nights when my father drove me back after my weekends at home and then deliriously happy for the rest of the week; and that we used to say a prayer before lunch each day to gentle Jesus to spare the little children in Europe. I cannot recall the slightest discomfort with my daily prayer to baby Jesus. I must have felt as legitimate as the next child in this exercise.

When I turned ten my mother thought it would be a good idea to upgrade my social education and I was accordingly enrolled as a boarder at Kambala, one of Sydney's leading ladies' colleges. Here I was in the company of daughters of the Australian aristocracy. It was the furthest point on the social ladder from my background of poor "Polka Yids" (Polish Jews) in the process of improving their financial lot in the open market-places of their new world. The cards were stacked against me in every conceivable way: reffo, Jew and trade! As far as I knew I was the only Jewish child in the whole school of some 400 pupils. If there were others, I was not aware who they were. I must have been a total misfit. The teachers' pets were the children of the most illustrious families. Many of the girls knew each other from the closed social ranks of their aristocratic families. Nonetheless I was reasonably happy and tried my best to fit in. I made no special friends, but I was not unduly isolated. I think my parents anonymity in the Sydney social scene was probably a far worse handicap than my Jewishness. Not that the other children knew I was Jewish. I made no reference to it or maybe I even hid it. I have forgotten.

I sang the hymns in Church as heartily as the next girl. I learnt to fear God and especially the Holy Ghost and looked for him each night under my bed before going to sleep and beseeching Gentle Jesus to care for me throughout the night. I believed in Jesus and he became my constant companion and comfort against the Holy Ghost who frightened the wits out of me. Each night at 7 o'clock I was shut up alone in the enormous assembly hall for my hour of piano practice. The piano faced a wall and behind me on the rostrum sat Jesus in one high-backed chair, God in another and finally the Devil in the guise of the Holy Ghost in a third. I used to agonise through my hour of piano practice in a cold sweat of fear until one night I hit upon the idea of moving Jesus' chair to the side of the piano where I could see him and he could better defend me against the Holy Ghost.

As my belief in Jesus grew, I took to arguing his cause with my father on my weekends at home. My parents requested that I be exempted from church attendance at school. I was bewildered and angered by this move. I had enjoyed the church service and especially the hymn-singing and saw my exemption as an expulsion. Furthermore, I was now marked as Jewish, a rejector of Christ, as clearly as if they had stuck a Star of David round my neck or printed the Mark of Cain upon my forehead.

I do not know whether I was treated differently from the other children, but I do know that at some stage in my second year I first became suspicious that this might be the case. Sitting one day in class, I raised my hand to ask to be excused. The teacher was inspecting exercise books one by one as we each finished some assignment and there was a queue of six or seven children waiting silently by her table. She did not look up for several minutes so I got up from my desk and went directly to her as I had left the matter till rather late, no doubt anxious to finish my assignment with the others.

"Excuse me for interrupting, Miss."

She looked up at me saying:

"Go to the end of the line and wait your turn like everyone else."

I waited in torment, knowing I would not be able to contain myself long enough to reach the head of the queue. I debated whether to try breaking ranks again or simply to go to the toilet without permission. In the event I did neither but stood there smiling nervously at the girl ahead of me as I felt the hot liquid beginning to seep down my stockings till finally it was too late to do anything. I crouched down, as the enormous pool of urine spread silently over the immaculate brown linoleum floor. I got up and snuck round to the back of the teacher's table. The lower half of my body was freezing,

"Excuse me Miss, I'm sorry but I couldn't wait".

"Wait for what?" This time she looked up at me.

"I couldn't wait to be excused" I whispered.

"So?" she bellowed,

"So I went on the floor!" I was pale and shaking in my soaking shoes.

"Where?" she said rising from her chair.

By now the whole class was staring at me. I led her to the dreaded spot. One of the girls, who had since joined the queue, was now standing in the middle of my puddle. She squealed and jumped aside.

"Why couldn't you put up your hand in time like everyone else?" yelled the teacher.

"Alright, alright already. So I'm not like everyone else" a voice was screaming inside my brain:

"Everyone else knew what to do and when to do it. Everyone else had parents who knew about gentle Jesus and his Virgin mother. Everyone else had been cleansed of human guilt and human dirt through Him, so of course everyone else would know the right time to put up her hand to be excused."

I stood there covered in shame with a great big yellow Star of David weighing on my heart. I knew what they must all be thinking.

By the end of the year my proclivities for the Christian religion were worrying my parents and with the headmistress's blessing I was removed from Kambala and sent to the local Bellevue Hill state school. Here there was a smattering of Jewish children - enough to fill our own religious instruction class on Wednesday mornings. But my friends were, in the main, non-Jewish children and no barriers of which I was aware divided us because of my Jewishness.

But much of which I was not aware at that time, did. One day in my last year of primary school, I asked one of my friends if she thought that the Jews were God's chosen people. I have long forgotten what prompted such a question. I guess it must have been a Wednesday, the day we had our weekly Bible class. But I remember vividly the hour and place of this small but unforgettable conversation. My friend's name was Jeanette. She was a prototype of Australian girlhood - robust and sturdy yet retaining the delicate porcelain complexion of her English forbears, overlain now with a healthy sprinkling of freckles. Her blond crinkly hair was plaited, and the thick shiny braids were always forward, displaced slightly by the pubescent burgeoning of her incipient bosom. I remember the emotional charge I felt in my question as I asked it half rhetorically, with pride, seeking confirmation by my school mate of my newly discovered biblical eminence as a member of God's "Chosen People". It was my first encounter with the idea that perhaps it was not only we Jews who believed that we were better than everyone else. I was sure of her answer, I wanted only to revel in it. There was no animosity or religious antagonism in my question, simply a childish showing-off. I waited with inflated pride for the touch of the good fairy's wand which would pronounce me a princess of royal descent.

With one sentence she shot her deadly venom-tipped arrow into my heart and froze the moment in my memory forever:

"You were God's Chosen People once" she said, "but not anymore."

All this happened at 3:50 p.m. on a hot summer afternoon in 1944 between the turn into the street where we both lived and her house. Jeanette had six sisters and no brothers and her uncle and aunt whom I never met, had six sons and no daughters. She lived just five houses from me and there were no other children of my age in the street. I was an only child and would have dearly loved to be able to play in her house with so many children around, but I never saw the inside of that house in the ten years we lived there. Nor did she ever come to my house. I never questioned this. I just accepted it.

I also never asked why we were no longer God's Chosen People. Nor did I ask anyone else. The conversation was relegated to my private store of unmentionable embarrassments for thirty-five years till I was reminded of it by the following passage in an essay by the Jewish American philosopher, H.M. Kallen:

"The Christian meaning of the word "Jew" rests on the interpretations of the New Testament by Orthodox

sectarian theologies. The sects differ widely among themselves. But to all alike "Jew" conveys the idea of being separated out, of a special people that had been first chosen and then rejected, a people cast by God for the role of villain in the drama of mankind's salvation. The plot of this drama is well known – the fall from grace of Adam and Eve in the Garden of Eden and their expulsion from Paradise to suffer the miseries of the human condition. Their sin was to be hereditary and constitutive and the destiny of their children and -- their children's children was to be eternal death, unless God's mercy tempered His justice and the First Parents' sin could at one and the same time be both expiated and forgiven. God's providence arranged human history toward this end. From among all the descendants of Adam he chose the seed of Abraham to be the vessels of His will. They only were to be His people; He only was to be their God. He revealed to them his commandments. He established them in the Promised Land. He raised up David to be King over them. Though they sinned much and were chastened much, He promised them a Messiah who in the fullness of time should save them." He came in the form of a Jewish man, Jesus of Nazareth, God's own begotten son. His death on the cross was the expiration of the sin of Adam. Those who believed in it were to be saved from the eternal death which was the consequence of that sin. Those who did not believe were to be cast out from the fellowship of the Saved. God's Chosen People, the Jews, did not believe. They regarded Jesus as a false Messiah; they rejected him, and they condemned him to the shameful death upon the cross. Thereupon God rejected them. They became the outcasts from the fellowship of mankind.

It is difficult if not impossible for any individual indoctrinated in childhood in the concept of Jews as deicides, Christ-killers, as rejected people, to think of the word "Jew" without discomfort and repulsion."

I remembered only after reading this that Jeanette father was a Methodist minister. As with every other emerging awareness of my Jewish identity in peaceful Australia I could never be sure of my interpretation of events. Was I excluded from the Jeanette's household because my ancestors had murdered the son of God? Or was I never invited to play inside the house because her Mother already had so many children she didn't know what to do. Perhaps Jeanette never came to my house because she had enough siblings to play with, or perhaps she simply didn't like me very much? Perhaps...

It occurred to me also after reading Kallen's essay that while I had all my life conveniently dissociated the Jews from those bad Jews in the New Testament who had screamed "Kill him, kill him" and retained only my connection with the good ones such as Moses and the prophets in the Old Testament, the Christians had done the reverse. To Jeanette I was not only the descendant of that blood-thirsty mob that had condemned Gentle Jesus to death, but I was also conveniently cut off from my legitimate heritage, the Old Testament. As we were no longer God's Chosen People we had also lost our special relationship with the good guys in the Bible like Moses and the prophets.

As I matured, I became progressively more suspicious of the prevalence of anti-Semitism in the society in which I was growing up. I have since encountered Jews who see anti-Semitism everywhere and those who see it nowhere. This problem was less for children growing up in overtly anti-Semitic societies than it was for us in Australia. There were many Christian homes in which I did play happily throughout my early childhood and the idea that I had been barred from the Jeanette's household because I was Jewish never entered my head…until now.

Then, quite unexpectedly, something happened which would forever resolve my doubts about my acceptance in Australian society. The thing itself was trivial and can only be understood in terms of its meaning to the child who experienced it. To me, at that time, it was a world-shattering experience.

I had, along with some twenty other Jewish children throughout the city, gained a place at Sydney Girls High School, in those days the top academic school in the city. Places were awarded strictly on merit to the top students from all the Sydney primary schools. I had been preparing for my first day of high school all through the twelve weeks of the summer vacation with as much excitement as a bride for her wedding day. I reviewed my new uniform, my first ever, with pride: brown tunics, one summer, one winter; three gleaming white shirts; the brown felt hat with its gold band; three pairs of brown knee-high socks and, above all, the gold and brown striped tie which would signify to all and sundry that I belonged to the most prestigious high school in Sydney; not one where my parents had to pay, but one where by my own achievements I had gained entry.

I rose to dress at 6 a.m. My hair washed the day before, shoes shined, clothes laid out, I was so well-rehearsed that I was all set to go by seven. The hours dragged till mid-day when at last we left the house for the most important interview of my life.

At Sydney Girls High School there were four classes in each year, designated from A to D, in descending order of merit. Of the one-hundred and twenty new students who had gained entry that year to the most academically prestigious high school in Sydney, twenty were Jewish. Accompanied by our mothers we were interviewed individually by the headmistress and told to which class we had been assigned. By the end of that catastrophic day, not one of the twenty Jewish girls had been assigned to the A class. One would have naturally assumed that, just as admittance to the school was gained strictly on merit, so too was the allocation to classes in the first year. However rightly or wrongly, I now concluded that the assignment to classes in the first year had not been determined on merit.

The headmistress announced without looking up from her papers that I was assigned to 1C. I was devastated as much for the impact this would have on my parents as for myself. The importance of academic achievement by their children to Jewish immigrants from Poland and Russia is not easily grasped by today's generation. The impact on me must have been comparable to that of the infamous numerus clausus* on our parents.

Two Jewish girls had made it into 1B, but as fate, or otherwise, would have it, their mothers spoke English without a foreign accent. It could conceivably be that the principal had made a considered judgment based on this very factor; that these children would be better able to cope academically because of the Anglo-Saxon background at home. But I did not, or could not, think rationally on the events of that day. It was for me a blinding tragedy; "Numerus Clausus*" Aussie style!

My schizophrenic ambiguity regarding, Jew and Gentile, was finally over. I was now sure that they did not want us, but merely tolerated us. I decided that the good life for Jews in Australia was not the product of a just and democratic society. Nor was it due to the lack of virulent European anti-Semitism. It was simply the by-product of the lowest common denominator compatible with Australia's own chosen comfortable standards of law and order. To tamper with exam results was not "British cricket", but to interpose the principal's judgment was.

The 1A class was filled with blond, blue-eyed, guileless, sporting Aussies. I looked upon them as belonging

numerus clausus: **A law limiting the number of Jews allowed to enter institutions of higher education.**

to a master-race. I remember once surreptitiously touching one of them with the tips of my fingers, as if by that ritual a little of the magic might rub off on me. I regarded myself with shame and winced each morning as I had to pass by the A and B rooms to my own resented, miserable part of the world.

The following year eleven of the twenty Jewish girls who had entered Sydney High that year had gained entry to the 2A class, allocation having reverted to published exam results.

Of course it is quite possible that my interpretation of these events may not be correct. But it is not relevant to this tale whether they are or not. Rightly or wrongly I was convinced that I had been discriminated against because I was Jewish. And in strong support of my conviction, the cold facts remain that based on the headmistress' own discretion not one out of the twenty Jewish girls that had entered Sydney High that year had been allocated to the 1A class. But on the very next exam for which results were made public, eleven of the Jewish girls had qualified for the 2A class.

I hated my first year of high school and deliberately isolated myself from the other children. It was a year of dark eclipse, but in 1946 the sun burst through again for me. From the day I walked into that 2A classroom my enthusiasm for life returned. I could again hold my head up high and believe in my own ability. My persecution complex of the previous year had been a private matter which I did not discuss with anyone. But what the other Jewish girls in my year had made of this situation may be gauged by the fact that no sooner did the eleven of us find ourselves in 2A the following year, than we banded together into a tight-knit social group which endured, with additions and subtractions, throughout our remaining four years of high school. In the playgrounds of Sydney Girls' High School in the years from 1946 to 1949, at the lunchtime break any day of the week, was to be found a small group of Jewish girls; the "Jewish Group" the others called us.

All the members of the group were born in Australia. English was our mother tongue. Physically most of us were not identifiable as Jews, a mixed bag of blonds and brunettes. None of us had ever experienced overt anti-Semitism. I have often wondered whether it was the shock of the Judenrein 1A experience that gave rise to the "Jewish Group", or perhaps the recent revelations of the Jewish genocide which had just taken place in Europe or a combination of both. Or was it just a coincidental consequence of our maturing political awareness?

The "Jewish Group"

In contrast to us Australian born Jewish girls, the Jewish refugee girls did not join the "Jewish Group". They were the daughters of German Jews, themselves born in

Germany, who had arrived in Australia in 1938 just before the outbreak of WWII. They were, on the whole, swarthier, slightly accented and easily identifiable as Jews. While we Australian born Jewesses, who had the choice of identifying ourselves as Jewish or not, were now choosing to define ourselves unambiguously as Jewish, these foreign-born girls sought to identify themselves as Australians of the Mosaic faith, just as their parents had tried to be Germans of the Mosaic faith. Without understanding it, I felt the hypocrisy of their situation. I regarded them as traitors.

The All Married Jews

Of the "Jewish Group" those that married all married Jews - some twice over. Some accentuated their Jewish identification in the typical Diaspora patterns of affiliation with Jewish philanthropical organizations, synagogue memberships and social clubs. Others have proceeded slowly along the paths of assimilation into the Gentile world and have to date, found little to impede their progress.

In retrospect the "Jewish Group" was a strange phenomenon. We all knew we were Jewish, but none of us knew precisely what that meant. We knew practically nothing of the history, religion, literature, culture, or even the traditions of the Jewish people. Yet, against all odds we were still there in 1947 as an identifiable group.

I know full well that much of what I have been telling here was my own subjective interpretation of those events. They must have been viewed quite differently by others, even in our group. However, the fact remains: a group of exclusively Jewish girls sat down together each day to eat lunch, voluntarily separating themselves from everyone else. Even the place chosen was tucked away out of sight and hearing of the other playing areas. At least some of the teachers must have noticed this. I wonder now what they thought of it. Certainly none ever made any attempt to tamper with the situation. It was fully accepted as part of the scene.

The 1C episode was critical in my evolving self-identification. Because of it I was now convinced that I really had no choice in the matter: that the society in which I was living discriminated against me because I was Jewish and there was nothing I could do to change that. I was born Jewish and that's what I would always be no matter how I felt about it

I moved from the blackest of miseries to the heights of euphoria at the age of 13 when I entered my second year at high school in the 2A class. If I sought an explanation for my euphoria, I must have believed that it was my promotion from the ignominious 1C class to the prestigious 2A class. However, today I believe the explanation operated at a much deeper level. The 1C episode persuaded me that the society in which I lived did not regard me as one of them. I was unambiguously Jewish and from that time on, the ambiguity of my self-identification would no longer trouble me. I now looked out on the world from a Jewish universe: all my friends were Jewish, I joined Jewish clubs where we sang Israeli songs and danced Israeli dances and I started to dream the Zionist dream.

CHAPTER 3:

SHYLOCK'S DAUGHTER

Having discovered that I didn't **always** have the option of being like other Australians when I chose to, I set about being Jewish all the time. The first step was to learn to like it. This was not as easy in 1946 as it would be today. Nobody seemed to like the Jews and it was not then even necessary to pretend to. Even my own image of the Jew was not entirely free of the legacy of mediaeval Christian European anti-semitism: an ugly, hook-nosed, servile, greedy groveler. Deciding to be Jewish all the time is a simple enough matter outwardly: all that is needed is to hang a Star of David around one's neck.

But that is not what I had in mind. It was my own denigrated image of the Jew and my inner conflict over the deliberate concealment or revelation of my Jewishness that I had decided to put an end to.

Before the war, anti-Semitism was part of the general xenophobia in Australia directed against all foreigners. But after the war, the government launched a campaign to increase the population of Australia by promoting European, especially British, immigration. Immigrants hitherto commonly referred to as "bloody reffos" now became "new Australians".

But Jewish immigrants were not generally accepted in the public psyche as "new Australians". In a poll conducted by the Melbourne University in 1948 to rate the relative popularity of foreigners immigrating to Australia, the Jews were ranked second last on the list of 14 different nationalities, with the Negroes coming last. Fifty-eight percent of the sample of 400 white-and-blue collar workers voted to bar all further Jewish immigration to Australia compared to thirty-one percent who were against all further German immigration and this just three years after the German genocide of European Jewry!

Not being readily identifiable as Jewish, if I did not deliberately and often inappropriately reveal my Jewishness early in a relationship, I ran the risk of exposing my companions to the embarrassment of revealing any anti-Semitic proclivities. On the other hand, if I deliberately made a point of exposing my Jewishness I appeared paranoid on this subject usually ruining any chances of a worthwhile interaction anyway. The net result was to abandon the enterprise entirely. Non-Jews were henceforth to be kept at a comfortable distance.

Coming to terms with my Jewishness inwardly was far more complicated. I had grown up in a world in which it was both the greatest pride and the greatest shame to be Jewish. I thought that not only Jews but everyone else believed that we were the cleverest people on earth. I had internalized the image of the Jew as intellectually superior, but I had also internalized his debased physical and moral image. Western standards of beauty, courage, fair play, and charity were Christian qualities.

If you were dark and good-looking, you were Italian. If you were dark and not good-looking, you were Jewish. I assigned the defects of my body and character to my Jewishness; my knock-knees and pubertal acne, my dismal performance in sports and anything else I was unsure about were all due to my Jewish genes.

There was to be no delegation of this problem to some more convenient time. In the first week of our second year back at school, we learned that our exciting initiation into the glories of Shakespeare was to be "The Merchant of Venice". The choice of this play for a class comprising thirty percent Jewish children, at the very time that the horrors of the concentration camps of Auschwitz and Dachau were being revealed has long intrigued me. Harold Bloom one of the most renowned Shakespearean critics of the 20th century, wrote of this play:

"One would have to be blind, deaf and dumb not to recognise that Shakespeare's grand equivocal comedy *The Merchant of Venice* is nevertheless a profoundly anti-Semitic work"

I have since discovered that "The Merchant of Venice" was commonly chosen as the first Shakespearean play taught in many high schools in many countries. I have never been certain, as with the class assignments of girls in our first year of high school, whether this was due to anti-Semitism or whether, in fact, *The Merchant of Venice* is for some good pedagogic reason a suitable introduction to Shakespeare.

But for me as a fourteen-year-old girl, the play grated on my raw Jewish complexes all year. I came to loathe the approach of that English lesson (thank God it occurred only once a week) as I had loathed the approach to the 1 C classroom. I had several problems with "The Merchant of Venice". I could not see in Shylock or Jessica much resemblance to any Jews I knew. Vengeance is the key to Shylock's character, but vengeance is not a Jewish trait. Shakespeare probably knew this, because into the mouth of Shylock he put the words:

"If a Christian wrong a Jew, what should be his sufferance by Christian example? Why, vengeance! The villainy you teach me, I will execute".

The theme of vendetta is not part of the Jewish heritage. The Jews could not have survived if they had spent their energies repaying Christian injustices. "An eye for an eye" and "a tooth for a tooth" in the Hebrew Bible have been wrongly interpreted by non-Jews as an ethical rather than a legal injunction. This primitive Biblical decree prescribes that when determining the penalty for crimes of men against men the punishment should be commensurate with the crime and has nothing to do with vengeance. The real explanation of Shakespeare's central characterization of the Jew as vengeful is, in my opinion, projection of Christian vengeance against the Jew for the spilling of Christ's blood. The "not one (more) drop of Christian blood" theme of Portia's defence of Antonio, supports this interpretation.

A second problem of Shylock's character for me was his miserliness. The image of this old man, hysterically clinging to his ducats and his money bag, did not reflect the people I saw about me at home. By this time, my parents and their friends were, on the whole, comfortably middle class. They had arrived there by hard work, thrift and prudence. Money was not an end to them, but a means. They spent liberally in comparison with non-Jews of equal wealth. As their positions improved, the Jews I knew enjoyed their money and gave liberally to those less fortunate than themselves. They did not hoard it and count it. True, there was amongst our parents an exaggerated concern with security and money which represented survival. But for Shylock, money is the object of itself. I saw it as clearly identifiable with Freud's subconscious connection of faeces with money and it dirties the man from top to toe. Shylock lives with, and for, his money. It is his main preoccupation, apart from thinking of his vengeance against Antonio. It fills not only Shylock's conscious, but also his subconscious mind:

"There is some ill a brewing towards my race, for I did dream of moneybags tonight" and his only use for money is: "to make it breed".

We were informed that the "Merchant of Venice" was a comedy; according to some critics, the finest one of all. As a comedy, Shakespeare must have intended that the central theme of the play be the love story, in which Shylock the Jew is but the foil in whom most of the unresolved elements of the comedy are concentrated and with whose elimination, they are finally resolved, following the general pattern of his early comedies. But all I could feel in it was the tragedy of my people which, at this very time, had just passed through their greatest catastrophe. To me Shylock was the scapegoat ultimately reduced to a whimpering idiot. His fate mirrored that of the pitiful skeletons emerging from Hitler's concentration camps. He is systematically stripped of everything he possessed, up to that ultimate of mediaeval Christian joys, his Jewishness. His final response, like that of the "mussel men" of Auschwitz, is not to feel anything anymore at all. Having lost his daughter, his ducats, his self-respect and finally his identity, Shylock's only salvation was to become a Christian. Totally annihilated **"he exits content"**!

I saw in the play a confirmation of my own innermost forebodings about my Jewishness. I was tormented to find that the man acclaimed as the greatest literary penetrator of the human psyche confirmed my own secret view that Judaism versus Christianity is dark versus light, just as I had experienced the dark unspeakable Jewish war and brilliant exciting Christian war we had just passed through:

"There is more difference between thy flesh, Shylock and hers (Jessica's, who has rejected her Judaism and converted to Christianity) than between jet and ivory". says Salarino to Shylock.

Like the identification of my own physical and character defects with my Jewishness, for Shakespeare goodness, kindness, generosity, mirth and happiness are only Christian virtues throughout the play and their inverse, therefore, Jewish:

"The Hebrew will turn Christian, he grows kind." mocks Antonio of Shylock.

The defect of the Jew is explicitly genetic, exactly as I felt it to be for me. Lancelot tells Jessica in one of the high comedy spots of the play that her only hope is that:

"Your father got you not, that you are not the Jew's daughter."

"That were a kind of bastard hope indeed" replies Jessica, "so the sins of my mother should be visited upon me"

"Truly, then, I fear you are damned by both father and mother", Lancelot concludes.

It was Jessica, like myself the daughter of a Jew, that disturbed me most. With his opening shot, Shakespeare penetrated the deadliest secret of a thirteen- year old girl, three hundred years later, on the other side of the world:

"Alack, what heinous sin is it in me to be ashamed to be my father's child".

I could not recognise anything, Jewish in Jessica: no conflict, no dark and light, no inside and outside, only bland, unidimensional Christian goodness. Shakespeare solved Jessica's Jewish problem by extirpating her Jewishness, while I was solving mine by extirpating my Christianness.

"The Merchant of Venice" entered my life at a critical period in the development of my Jewish identity. Because of this, it had an enormously exaggerated effect on me. I came to it with all the eagerness of pubescent youth, hungry for experience and knowledge. At thirteen, one's first Shakespearean play is almost an initiation rite into the adult world of literature. I left it as stunned and hurt as a disappointed wallflower, at her first ball.

From the advantage of years and having reread it many times, I believe the play, for all the whitewashing that it has received, to be a profoundly anti-Semitic work, superbly subtle and effective from the pen of the master. With strokes of genius he paints a canvas in which the brilliance of the Christian character does as much to darken that of the Jew as does his direct portrayal of the Jew as the very "devil incarnate from which every good creature flees".

Historically, Shylock has dominated the play, no matter what Shakespeare originally intended. So profound is the Jewish impact (anti-Semitic or not) of the play that Shylock is, almost universally mistaken for the Merchant of Venice, despite the fact that the dramatis personae clearly states that Antonio is the only Merchant of Venice in this play.

The contention that the play is anti-Semitic is challenged by many with Shylock's famous plea for compassion. In the entire, unabated diatribe against the Jew, this one famous redeeming speech is acclaimed by Jewish and non-Jewish scholars alike to demonstrate Shakespeare's appreciation of the suffering Jewish soul. Taken at face value, without searching for a rebuttal of the anti-Semitic nature of the play, the only message of this speech is that although evil, miserly, mean-spirited, disgusting and stupid, the Jew is, nevertheless, of the human species. The famous questions prefaced by "Hath not a Jew?" are but bare bones thrown to a hungry dog. They do not question why the Jew deserves to be tortured, but only that by being human the Jew suffers if tortured. All that can be claimed for this speech, in my opinion, is that Shakespeare, unlike the Nazis, did not seek to exclude the Jews from the human race.

I emerged from these experiences with my Jewish identity clearly and irrevocably implanted. My knowledge of Judaism at this time was practically nil, but my gut view of myself and where I belonged in this world was now locked into my mind and probably will be forever. Since then, even in my dreams I am Jewish.

CHAPTER 4:

THE EXTINGUISHED SPARK

As a child in Australia the war in Europe affected me in contradictory ways: it frightened but also excited me. I sometimes wondered how different it must have been to have been a child when there was no world war. I was seven years old when the war started and thirteen when it ended. I kept a tally of the number of allied and enemy planes shot down as reported in the newspapers each day. It was like a cricket match to me and I barracked fervently for our side. But I also felt guilty for my enjoyment of this excitement.

I never felt anxious for my own safety, but I sometimes wondered if my parents did. I have often wondered since then how I might have felt had I been a parent at that time and at this thought I feel intense anxiety. I cannot understand now how they carried on so calmly. I wonder why in 1942 when it looked as though Hitler would win the war we didn't move to another city where no one knew we were Jewish and prepare a Christian identity for ourselves. I have never heard of anyone who did. Yet the Australian government was circumspect enough to destroy all records of Jewish identification (which in retrospect I find surprising, but admirable given the extent of anti-Semitism prevalent in Australia at that time).

Before the war ended, I already knew that Jews were being exterminated in Europe, but I did not feel real emotion at this horror. I did sometimes feel guilty because of this but on the whole, I accepted everything that was happening in Europe as the way things were. Whatever it was, it was like some nebulous tornado happening on the other side of the world and had been happening as long as I could remember. I could not recall a time in my young life when it had not been happening.

Some months after the war ended a telegram arrived at our house which read:

"Necha et Thomas deportés. Maurice et Simon chez nous. Bella et Abram".

My mother became hysterical. She flung herself on her bed and howled and screamed. I was frightened out of my wits. It must have been her release from the years of pent-up anxiety and guilt over her family caught in Hitler's death trap - her father, two sisters and a brother with their entire families. Like the symbolic tearing of clothes, she pulled at her hair and beat her breasts fiercely. I cowered in my room till her fury abated and then crept into her bedroom to try to comfort the convulsive impervious creature prostrated on the bed.

I was bewildered by her reaction. I thought that we had expected no survivors and the telegram had brought us four. I sat there on the floor in silence for hours waiting for her to return. From time to time I tried to tell her that the telegram had brought good news, not bad, but to no avail. It was to be our day of inconsolable mourning. My father led me gently away and we left her there to work it out for herself.

Meanwhile he sat at the dining room table with his head between his hands and stared, probably at the faces of his mother and sister and brother and their families from whom no telegram had come. I wandered from room to room in the silent house experiencing my first real encounter with the Holocaust.

A few months later the first letters started arriving from my aunt and uncle in Paris. The story was soon pieced together. Necha and Thomas, Simon's and Maurice's parents had been deported to Auschwitz in 1942. The children, who had witnessed their parents' arrest had fled to their aunt and uncle's house and the four of them had escaped together to the South of France where they had hidden amongst the peasants for the duration of the war. That was all I ever learnt about their experiences during the Holocaust and it has never struck me till this moment how bizarre this fact is. I have since heard the experiences of dozens of people who survived the Holocaust but not from my own family. Like sex it was something to learn about outside the house.

Despite the fact that there were not that many of them left, the entry of Jews into Australia was heavily restricted after the War. We applied immediately for entry visas for our pitiful quota of survivors and waited months for a reply. When at last it came, it took yet another year to obtain passages on a boat. In the meantime I had started corresponding with my cousin Maurice who had been teaching himself English in preparation for his forthcoming immigration. He was seventeen years old, handsome as a film star - he looked like Lesley Howard (who I learnt years later was also Jewish) - and for me he had arisen like some phoenix, out of that burning bush where none of us had dared to look. He knew things that no one I had ever met knew. He was also the first boy who had even spoken to me since the age of eight or nine. I was thirteen and entering puberty.

This combination of circumstances must have sparked the flame which soon developed into my first 'crush'. The distance and the waiting only enhanced my obsession with this pen-pal. I thought of little else. I wrote poems to his picture. The characteristic smell of the low-grade paper on which his letters were written was like Channel No.5 to my eager senses. For a whole year I fell asleep each night reliving my imagined meeting with him when that boat carrying him to me would finally sail into Sydney Harbour.

I was fifteen and he nineteen when the longed-for moment arrived. It was a brilliant Sydney summer's day. I stood away from the crowds huddling at the far end of the jetty, trying to catch their first glimpse of loved ones as the boat docked. My heart pounded as the ship drew closer. People shouted as they recognized relatives and wept for those who would never be seen again.

The wharf-laborers who, like me, had moved back from the milling crowd, caught my attention. They had probably never seen a bunch of Jews before, certainly none rocked by the emotional convulsions that they were witnessing now. They had stopped work to watch the show and stood there, arms folded above their swollen beer-bellies looking down superciliously on the weird mob below. My stomach tightened at the sight of them. We **were** a weird mob. Few spoke English without an accent and now we were also exposing our secret Jewish joys and sorrows in the full glare of a bright Australian summer's day, instead of in the gloom of our shuttered dining rooms to which they were normally confined. I was glad that I was not standing down there amongst that herd and furious with myself for feeling ashamed of them.

I had kept my mother in view in the crowd, expecting her recognition to guide me to our family. Now, when I looked back at her I saw them! My cousins were in heavy tweed knickerbocker trousers with matching jackets, quite inappropriate to the hot day and bizarre, to say the least, in the conformist anti-fashion milieu of Australian manhood. Had they appeared at school in them they would have been lynched on their first day.

My stomach tightened a little further. Instead of the pride I should have been feeling in my first ever boyfriend (even though he didn't yet know it). I suddenly wanted to hide him in his tweed knickerbockers up in the *boidem* or down in the *kaila* along with all the other tell-tale clues of my foreign origins.

I banished these uncomfortable thoughts with a determined smile at the wharfies and bounded down to join the crowd already moving to the exit of the customs house. A few of the immigrants were intermittently appearing at the open siding of the huge customs warehouse, trying to find their relatives outside. Some customs officials moved swiftly to stop them.

"Get back!" one shouted, "yers not allowed to talk t' anyone outside this warehouse."

The bewildered survivors hesitated a moment and not understanding a word he had said, resumed their conversations in Yiddish with those at the front of the crowd outside. The officials moved in and started to shove them back from the opening.

"Don't touch them" I heard myself yelling. "Haven't they been through enough?" A path opened ahead of me in the crowd and I was encouraged to move forward to the front. The customs officials had stopped pushing the new arrivals and turned to see what the commotion was about.

"You must not touch those people. They don't understand what you're saying."

They were taken aback at the sight of a fifteen- year old girl challenging their authority and their hesitation buoyed me on.

"Then you tell 'em to get back" one ordered.

I was hoisted up onto the siding. I knew that it was my Australian accent that had challenged their authority to manhandle these "reffos" and not what I was saying. Instinctively I broadened it to match their own.

"What d'ye want me t'tell 'em?"

"Tell 'em there's rules against sayin' anything t' anyone outside this warehouse until they've cleared customs."

In broken Yiddish I started to translate as best as I could. As soon as they heard my broken Yiddish the survivors set upon me with kisses and hugs, not hearing a word of what I was trying to say. I was pulled hither and thither, one wanting to know if I'd seen his sister, another with a form he couldn't understand. The officials moved back into position and herded the lot of us back into the interior of the warehouse.

I was in! My heart started to pound. Where was Maurice? Now I was frightened because I would have to meet him all alone and I had counted on the others breaking the ice for me. I had wanted first to be noticed by my absence and then they would ask where I was and then I would make my appearance and my uncle and aunt and Simon would all embrace me heartily and after that Maurice and I would be introduced to each other as if for the first meeting of an arranged marriage. I would stand there radiant and blushing and he would approach slowly, dazed by his first glimpse of my devastating beauty. Carefully controlling the passion surging through his body, he would kiss me delicately on each cheek, French style and engage my eyes for a split second as he withdrew.

"Hélène, Hélène" I reeled round. It was Simon. He lifted me off the ground and whirled round with me in his arms. He was taller and heftier than Maurice. He put me down, took a firm grip of my hand and ran me across the hall to the others. "*Voici la petite*" he yelled to them. I was smothered in kisses, dishevelled and diminished. Maurice kissed me smack on the mouth like the others and rushed off to complete the customs formalities he alone could cope with.

I stayed for a little while, trying to communicate in my high school French and then excused myself to see if I could help Maurice with the customs officials. No longer Joan of Arc nor Elizabeth Taylor, whom I was supposed to look like, but 'la petite Hélène. I found him waiting his turn in a queue. Emotionally exhausted, I simply came up and stood silently beside him. Without a word he put his arms around me and squeezed me to him.

For the next three years I worshipped him. I lived for him, learnt for him, dressed for him and in my single bed I slept with him. He was never out of my mind. It was an obsession such as I have never experienced again. By the end of his first year in Australia he had passed the high school leaving certificate almost entirely by his own efforts both to learn English and compensate for his missed schooling. I thought he was a genius. Because it was not deemed wise for him to live in our house, me being such a nubile young maiden, he was housed first with my mother's older sister who had emigrated to Australia before the War and then with Aunty Bella and Uncle Abraham when they moved to their own apartment later in the year. A very determined effort was made to keep us apart as puppy love developed between us. I got to see him only once a week on Sundays. We would all assemble for lunch at one of the three sisters' homes. Maurice and I would distance ourselves from the others as soon as we could. If we all took a walk after lunch as we did in the summer months, he and I would walk on ahead holding hands. I wonder now how we dared do even that in the puritanical ethos of the times. I counted the days from Sunday to Sunday and my week revolved around our few hours of bliss together. He took me on wonderful adventures through science and poetry and politics. Even then he was political. He was a passionate communist. The science and poetry were always politically coloured - Lamarckian genetics and Soviet poetry. It really didn't matter - I hung on every word.

After a year and a half of our Sunday sessions we started going for short outings on our own to visit a friend or to an early movie. We would walk home together with arms around each other's waists, still discussing science and poetry.

At last one night, sitting on a bench in Vaucluse Bay, overlooking the moon-lit waters of Sydney harbour, he suddenly lurched forward and pressed a wet, sweaty kiss onto my mouth. The pressure was a little too hard and he hurt my lip with his teeth. My heart leapt up in my chest, I felt slightly sick as I suddenly realised that what was happening was what I had been yearning for since I had first discovered his existence three and a half years earlier.

Maurice took me to his Communist cell, but I never got him to my Zionist youth group. It was a silent resistance. He never opposed my Zionist proclivities. He just believed that the Jewish problem was part of the general constellation of the capitalist malaise which would disappear with the advent of his brave new world. I could not argue the case for my Zionism as he could for his Communism. I understood even then that his solution for the Jewish problem was the spiritual annihilation of the Jews. Instinctively I rejected it. But I knew nothing of the philosophy of Judaism, and he knew everything of the philosophy of Marxism.

Maurice represented to me a spark that Hitler had failed to extinguish, a surviving witness who might reveal something of our history that had been deliberately censored both by my parents and the world. But I learnt nothing about the Holocaust from him. He never mentioned what had happened to his parents. He never spoke to me about the war, except to mention some factual matter in passing and I never asked. I had been conditioned not to talk about "our" war during my childhood. But this had not prevented me from thinking about it. This taboo had imbued the Holocaust with a quality of mystique bordering on the supernatural. Maurice was a survivor of this formless terror which had so elusively and yet so traumatically clouded my childhood. I elevated him to the stature of a prophet. He knew things about our Jewish war that I could never know.

But Maurice did not even see himself as a Jew. As soon as he finished his education, he quickly disentangled himself from me and eventually from the entire family. After qualifying in psychiatry at Sydney University, he returned to Paris and married a lovely French Catholic peasant. He adopted her family as his own instead of ours. It was not the Catholic element that he sought in place of our Jewishness, but the proletarian class instead of our middle class. His wife wears a cross around her neck and that bothers him no more nor less than if she wore a Star of David.

But to my mother he represented the heritage bequeathed to her by her dead sister; the victory of life over death. She considered it her holy duty to assume the responsibility denied to his parents. She paid his way through university and lavished her time and affection on him. To her his marriage to a non-Jewish woman was a betrayal. Six million Jews had died in the Holocaust, including his parents and it was now up to the survivors to replace them. To my mother and many of the rest of the traumatised Jewish people, by marrying a non-Jewish girl Maurice was handing Hitler a posthumous victory.

CHAPTER 5

WHAT'S IN A FORESKIN?

I graduated from Sydney Girls High School in 1949, winning a prize for German! There was a rule that native German speaking students were not eligible to win this prize. But the authorities forgot or did not know that Yiddish comprises about 80% mediaeval German and so I suspect that Jewish students had been winning this prize for German for some years.

Apart from my first class honour in German, my matriculation results were pretty ordinary: one first class honour, one second class honour, three A's, one B and one failure. But that was sufficient in those privileged times to win a scholarship which entitled me to study for free at Sydney University. My parents were overjoyed at having lived to see an end to the dreaded Numerus Clausus of their youth.

I enrolled in the Science Faculty at Sydney University in 1950, focused more on the anticipated exciting social life than the education which lay ahead. .

During my first year I was introduced to the mysterious world of the Free Thought Society. Their meetings were more exciting than a ride on the big dipper at Luna Park. I had transferred my extinguished flame for Maurice to a young Jewish anarchist called Alwyn Karpin, a pimply nineteen- year- old who hung out at the university cafeteria with a group of disciples of the infamous Professor Anderson, head of the philosophy department. It was not their endless discussions which I rarely understood which intrigued me, but rather their anarchic, bohemian lifestyles. They lived in a number of communally shared rooms and apartments scattered around the sleazier suburbs of Sydney. Many, if not the majority of them, came from highly respectable well-to-do homes.

There was an inner core of fully committed members who were impoverished, dirty and in various stages of drug addiction and physical decay. But most of us simply enjoyed stepping out of our well-defined worlds of hum-drum middle class law and order into chaos.

Alwyn belonged to the inner core. I attached myself to him for protection as much as anything else. Being a Jew I felt that he would understand the terror and fascination that this new-found world inspired in me. He was flattered by the bevy of young Jewish girls from our "Jewish Group" who, like me, had made him their latest idol.

There was a considerable amount of "free love" going on around us and one by one the girls of the "Jewish Group" were losing their virginities. I too was eager to pass this new milestone, without which one could never qualify as *"avant-guard"*. In this world there were two distinct classes of people - those who did and those who did not engage in pre-marital sex. Those who did not engage in premarital sex supported establishment values and those who did opposed them. It was essential to cast off one's virginity to raise oneself above the common herd. Unfortunately for me, Alwyn, who despite his heavy dose of pubescent acne would have suited me admirably in this quest, evinced no interest in my obvious invitation. Instead I was passed on to his friend Darcy Waters, the prize stag of the Free Thought Society. Darcy looked as his name sounded, like an English cricketer; tall with wavy fair hair and a perfect complexion - a complete foil to the mousy spotted Alwyn. Darcy wooed me for several months: I was the envy of many a non-Jewish girl, most of them far prettier and certainly more sophisticated than me. What he saw in me I could not fathom. Perhaps it was the challenge of my rejections or the novelty of a dark Jewish soul though I could hardly believe I would be the first Jewess for this mighty Casanova. Whatever it was, my resistance strengthened his determination. He pursued me till he became the joke of the group. A lovelorn Darcy was a contradiction in terms!

One night in desperation a plan was laid to ensnare me. Four of us were to meet in Darcy's room at the "Cross" for drinks before going on to a party in Redfern, an inner industrial suburb of Sydney. Ten minutes after I arrived the other two, Alwyn and a girl, announced they were leaving and would see us later at the party. Before I could grasp what was happening, they disappeared out the door. Darcy plied me with alcohol and warmed quickly to the night's work. I decided the chips were down. I would try to relax and think of the Empire. The drunker I got the more I giggled; the closer he got the louder I giggled. Suddenly I saw fear in his eyes,

"For Christ's sake keep quiet" he begged. I've got a Catholic landlady".

So, the chips were not down after all; he had handed me a weapon with which to defend myself. I giggled on, but as I felt the change in his excitement moving from mental to physical, genuine terror overtook me and my giggling became uncontrollably hysterical. The Catholic landlady started banging on the door.

"Jesus fucking Christ" he groaned and gave up.

We rode to Redfern in stony silence on the upper level of a double decker bus. I felt miserable and guilty for having humiliated him. I was confused at my own behaviour. Why had I not gone through with it? I knew it had to be done. Most of my friends had already been deflowered, or so I believed, and Darcy was nothing to be ashamed of as an initiator. Yet I knew that I would do the same again if the occasion arose.

I began to sense my familiar feelings of fraud but for the first time in an entirely different context. Not the Jewess passing herself off as a Christian, but now a frigid square in the ranks of the avant-garde.

"I'm sorry," I whispered.

"Forget it. This should be a good party," he said deliberately avoiding further discussion of our fiasco. "Everyone's coming. There'll be quite a crowd"!

I had never been to a "Push" party before. The Sydney Push was a society of poets and artists in the late forties which together with Anderson's Free Thought Society comprised much of the disreputable non-conformist substructure of Sydney's intellectual life. The

"Push" parties were famous or infamous, according to one's attitude. One had to be invited and thereby vouched for by some existing member. Neither the Push nor the Free Thought Society were illegal organisations, but there had been frequent brushes with the law, especially at these infamous parties. Now I was being taken to one for the first time. Perhaps the planned seduction had been a pre-requisite to my admission.

We got out of the bus at the dismal Redfern shopping centre and walked down a squalid ill-lit working-class street of identical semi-detached Victorian cottages. It was a cold damp winter night and the street was deserted. When we reached our destination, Darcy pushed open the creaky garden gate and taking hold of my hand led me round by a side path to the back entrance to the house. Heavy brownish curtains were drawn across the front windows and from within came the muffled concentrated sounds of a dense crowd. The kitchen was strewn with empty wine and beer bottles and a few plates containing the remnants of peanut shells and cupcake paper containers. There was a couple leaning against the sink in animated conversation. Darcy led me on into the living room. It was lit by a single globe covered with a long-fringed 1920's lampshade. Visibility was almost nil, and it took several seconds for my eyes to adapt after the bright naked light of the kitchen.

Gradually I discerned the picture of what I perceived to be a world gone mad. It was not only my eyes that had needed a moment or two to adapt, but also my brain, to ascertain that I had not just walked through the looking glass into a lunatic asylum. There were couples cuddling on the sofas. Others, oblivious to them, were sitting or standing around engaged in deep philosophical conversations. Someone was throwing up in the corridor leading to the front door. I felt my knees giving way under me. Darcy moved to lead me through the corridor, past the vomiting drunk, to stairs leading to the floor above. I froze with terror. Suddenly I wanted to be back in Bellevue Hill with my mummy and daddy.

"Take me home, Darcy" I whispered.

"For Christ's sake" he snarled, "how much more of your fucking middle-class morality do I have to put up with to-night?"

He started to pull me after him. I disengaged my hand from his and ran into the backyard. I stood there for a couple of minutes hoping he would take pity and accompany me, at least, to the bus stop. Suddenly I heard raised voices coming from the kitchen.

"Leave her alone, I'll take her home". It was Alwyn coming to find me.

He put his arm around my waist and gently headed me towards the gate. The cold air cleared my head.

"You and Darcy planned this whole terrible evening, didn't you?" I challenged.

"Yes" he replied softly. "We thought it was what you needed".

"But why Darcy?" I asked, avoiding the implications of his remark.

"Why not?" he retorted, "He's really keen on you".

"But he's not even Jewish" was my knee-jerk response.

"What difference does that make?" he asked.

"I don't know. But you could have gotten me over the line this evening and he couldn't."

"How can you know that" he smiled, a little embarrassed at my boldness.

"Because you understood why I had to be taken home now and he didn't".

Non-Jewish boys stopped appearing at our house after that night. My parents never knew why, but I'm sure they welcomed the change. Thirty years later I was reminded of that night with Darcy when driving a nineteen-year old American girl back to her dormitory in the Old City of Jerusalem. It was late at night and the gates into the Old City were closed to traffic. I was a little concerned at leaving her to walk in the deserted alleyways alone.

"Don't worry," she said. "I'll just wait till I see a guy with a kippa(skull cap) and get him to walk me down to the dorms."

I understood what she meant: here in Jerusalem what a guy with a kippa signified for her was what a guy with a circumcised penis had signified for me in Australia: a common ancestry which had endowed us with a common understanding. Avant-garde guys without a foreskin were doing exactly the same things as avant-garde guys with one, but I felt safer with the latter because I knew the world they were transgressing and they knew the world to which I would have to return.

CHAPTER 6

ANTONIO'S SON

I was nineteen years old and savouring my first real taste of freedom. I had just completed my first year at university. I used to get up each morning intoxicated with the feeling that anything might happen before the day was out. New experiences, new people, new places, new ideas flooded in. Our little group split up and started out on divergent paths, to which we have all, surprisingly, more or less stuck ever since. Life has dealt us the whole gamut of its vagaries from early death and torment to contentment, fame and riches, but in those days we were blessed only with youth and eagerness.

Although most of us had danced and sung our way through the Zionist youth movements of Sydney, I was the only one ever to live in Israel. My first attempt in 1951 had little to do with ideology. It was simply part of the adventure of growing up and, more importantly, escaping the suffocating restrictions of an overprotective Jewish mother. I met a young man, a graduate in law, who at twenty-four had life all worked out. There was for Geoff only one of two paths as a Jew - assimilation or immigration to Israel. This was the prevailing doctrine of the young Jewish socialists. According to them, as we headed towards world communism, Jews would disappear into the classless society. Therefore, only Israelis and not Diaspora Jews would or should survive, as the continuation of the Jewish people.

Having completed his law course, Geoff's ambition was to pursue a political career. But on attempting to apply for a job in the diplomatic Corps, he was warned that Jews though not formally barred, were not encouraged to pursue careers in this area. Instead he opted for the alternative option to become an Israeli. Unlike most immigrants to Israel at this time, Geoff's motive for immigrating was to further the cause of socialism rather than Zionism.

But I was no more concerned about his socialism than I had been about Maurice's communism. I saw in Geoff firstly the opportunity to travel and secondly to acquire a husband. As I believed that the primary goal of a university course was finding a suitable husband, abandoning my prized free university education after only one year presented no problem.

For my requirements, Geoff could not have been bettered. Not only was he about to travel to Israel in order to remain a Jewish socialist in the new world order, but he hailed from an eminently desirable elite Australian Jewish family; one which would admirably fulfil my mother's aspirations in her adopted land. I grasped the opportunity. If I had a hope in Hades of gaining her permission to sally forth into that wide wonderful world beyond the ocean at Bondi beach, this was it. In those days hardly anyone travelled abroad, let alone an over protected nineteen- year old Jewish girl.

Geoff was a third generation Australian on his father's side and second on his mother's side. There was, I knew, an ambivalent reverence in us new immigrants for these old "Anglo-Saxon" Jews. They were by now no longer the wealthiest segment of Jewish society, but rather its unassailable aristocracy. Geoff's mother was a member of the Myer family (originally Baevski), founders of "Myers", the leading department store in Australia at that time. By now the Myer family had more Gentiles than Jews in it. Some, still clinging valiantly to their Jewish heritage, wanted their children to marry "in" but preferably amongst their own set of "Mayflower" Jews. For me to marry Geoff would undoubtedly be viewed by all as a step up for me and a step down for him. I may have conquered my ambivalences about my Jewishness in high school, but it was to take another decade for me to come to terms with my "Warsaw ghetto" origins. My future mother-in-law told me, at our engagement party, how pleased they were that Geoff was marrying me rather than some dark oriental Jewess he might meet in Israel!

Geoff left for Israel eight months ahead of me to blaze the trail. He would find a suitable kibbutz for us and I, meanwhile would toughen up a little for the rigors that lay ahead, in the recently established training camp (*Hagshara*) at Shepparton in Victoria, created for this very purpose. It was to be the beginning of my transformation from a spoilt Jewish Princess to an enlightened member of the proletariat.

Hagshara was great, one long extended Christmas camp. We had to work a fairly strenuous ten- hour day, picking peaches or working in the communal laundry or kitchen. But it was fun to be living with a group of young people and close to nature for the first time in my life.

I returned home a month before I was due to sail. This was 1951 and international travel was by sea. The journey to Israel would take a month. My ship, the *Neptunia* was on her maiden return voyage back to Italy. She had arrived packed with 1600 Italian immigrants in search of the good life I was leaving. There was little tourism in those days as Europe was still in ruins from the Second World War and so for the return journey to Italy there were now only 6 passengers!

For me that journey was a tale straight out of the Arabian Nights, complete with prince charming, full moons on tropical seas and weird exotic eastern ports. Amongst the six passengers was a blond Adonis called Marcello Baronci. He had been one of the 1600 immigrants on the *Neptunia's* maiden voyage to Australia. He took a brief look at Sydney and decided that Australia was not for him. He bought a return ticket and remained on board the Neptunia for the return voyage to Italy.

Our month on board was the stuff that dreams are made of. We were waited on like royalty. At night the ships band played just for the six of us and we danced away our month under tropical moonlit skies in a fairy tale never to be repeated. Disconnected from the planet, out of sight of land for weeks on end, Marcello and I floated together in an unreal world, oblivious to any fears or doubts that may have assailed us for the times that lay ahead, his in bankrupted Italy and mine in Israel.

Our shipboard romance culminated with Marcello invading my cabin on our last night at sea. He had come to consummate the affair. But as with Darcy a year earlier the attempt ended in chaos. I did not realise it then, but I think I was just unable to sleep with an uncircumcised man, just as many secular Jews cannot bring themselves to eat ham. We lay together in my berth all-night and watched for the first appearance of the Italian coast at dawn, that magic moment that I had dreamt of all my life! I had at last arrived "over there" in Europe, the home of all that history, literature, art and music that I had heard about all my life together with the unspeakable horrors of my childhood war.

I had a week to spend in Rome before I would have to board my next boat, the *Abbazia* for the last leg of the journey across the Mediterranean to Israel.

Marcello knew that I was Jewish and told me how good the Pope had been to the Jews during the war. He did not tell me what his father had been doing during the war. Nor did I ask. He took me home to meet his family and his mother told me, via his interpreting, that if he had only met a nice girl like me in Australia he might have been able to stay. Marcello and I chuckled at our silent joke under the multitude of crucifixes that bedecked his home!

The following day Marcello showed me Rome in a day. Touring the city on the passenger seat of his *vesperetta* we sped past most of the famous monuments, stopping only to take in panoramic views from one or other of the seven hill tops surrounding the city. Then on the way back to my hotel we suddenly stopped on route.

"Come I want to show you something" he said alighting from the motor scooter. We made our way on foot into the ruins of the ancient Roman Forum and came to rest in front of the magnificent Arch of Titus, a triumphal arch erected to commemorate the victory by the Romans in the War against the Jews in Judea in 70 C.E. Depicted on its walls are images of Jews in chains being brought back to Rome as slaves .

In those days, when tourists were still relatively sparse in Europe, the Pope granted small audiences for them once a week. Marcello arranged a pass for me but would not come with me. Why, I do not know to this day. He delivered me to the appropriate door in the Vatican and I joined a small queue of about fifty people waiting to be admitted. Next to me was a young woman from New York loaded with dozens of rosaries draped over the entire length of her outstretched arms. Once inside the receiving chamber the Pope blessed us in several languages and the audience in turn raised rosaries and babies high above their heads as they heard the blessing in their own language.

When we emerged, the woman from New York asked me what religion I was. I fumbled for an answer and haltingly answered, "Protestant". My school-girl feelings of fraud began to surface. What was I, a Jewess, doing in the 1A classroom?

"I am Jewish" she retorted,

" I have brought all these rosaries for Catholic friends from New York!"

I was shocked and humiliated at my own cowardice. Years later I was reminded of this shameful degrading incident when I saw a T-shirt in a Jerusalem shop window which defiantly proclaimed: "We did so kill Him" and on the back "So what?"

Marcello was my first and only experience of a close communion with a gentile boy. We parted with real affection and wonderful memories and never met or corresponded again. He has always remained my Catholic and I hope I am his Jewess - one brief encounter across that chasm which, we both well knew, irrevocably divided us.

CHAPTER 7

A MOUTHFUL OF WORMS

One week later back in Naples I boarded the Abbazia bound for Israel. For the first time since leaving Sydney I was beginning to register the gravity of the decision I had taken in abandoning my education, my home, my entire life up to this time. I was suddenly, for the first time since leaving Australia, utterly and totally alone.

The Abbazia was an old wreck of a boat. There was only one class - third. She was crowded with Jewish immigrants from South America. Many Nazi war criminals had found refuge in Argentina and this no doubt was responsible for the current exodus of Argentinian Jews. I knew nothing about these people. I didn't know where they'd come from. Were they native South Americans or displaced Europeans? Were they rich or penniless or a mixed bag? Some spoke English, but they were remote, turned in on themselves, weighed down with their own miseries. I immediately clicked into an alien stance: I and they.

There was one obvious difference between me and them; they were not voluntary immigrants to Israel as I was. This placed me in an unassailable position of superiority. *I* was the idealist coming to save *them*. They were not like the Jews I had known in Australia. They were uptight, secretive and aloof.

On our second day out at sea a well-dressed, rather corpulent gentleman struck up a conversation with me. It was obvious from his slow, relaxed, confident air that he was not one of *"them"*. He knew the crew, spoke fluent Hebrew and was aware of what was to come: how many days to Haifa and the procedures awaiting us there. He also smiled and cracked jokes and paid attention to other people. He was a man of about my father's age and spoke good English, and I soon came to feel at home with him.

He continued to seek me out over the next twenty-four hours till I finally waited for him to take our meals together. The following morning, about three hours before we were to dock at Cyprus, he told me that he was the harbour-master of Haifa port. He also told me that he had a private bank account in Cyprus and that if I liked I could give him whatever dollars I was carrying to deposit in his account there and that on arrival in Haifa he would repay me at the black market rate in Israeli pounds. I trusted him utterly and believed him when he said that my dollars would be useless if changed on the regular market in Israel as the Israeli lira was practically worthless.

I gave him my money and he did return it in Israeli liras at the black-market rate, which was 150% higher than the bank rate. But I was shattered! Corruption in the highest quarters of my Utopia, the Promised Land, for which I was so nobly sacrificing myself to help salvage the remnants of my ravished people! Already I too had been corrupted and I had a feeling that there was worse to come.

Our last night at sea was to match physically the emotional turbulences that were by now beginning to stir in me. I had always imagined the Mediterranean as a placid, blue ocean gently lapping away at the famous playgrounds of the rich. But now, as clouds began to gather above, I suddenly remembered the treachery that I had read of in some tattered book of Greek or Roman literature back in a sunny Australian classroom. It was late November in 1951 and we were sailing into a storm to rival anything ever recorded by the ancients. Our ship tossed rhythmically from side to side for hours on end. With each dip all the furniture, crockery, nautical trappings and many of the passengers, weakened with vomiting, rolled the complete width of the ship and back. By the morning there was not an un-smashed cup left from which to drink. The last thing we heard on the radio, before it too was smashed, was that a boat had sunk in Haifa harbour and seven people had drowned. But the storm provided an emotional release for me. I remember feeling no fear or panic, but rather a slightly hysterical euphoria as I lay on my bunk and imagined what it must have been like to be rocked as a baby in a cradle.

We docked at Haifa port under a miserable grey sky at 7a.m. the following morning. The rain had stopped, but everything was damp and the ground looked waterlogged. I don't recall my first glimpse of the Holy Land. My only lasting memory is the shock of my first glimpse of Geoff. I waved heartily and put on a brave smile, but inside I cringed. A lump rose in my throat and I was glad that at least at that moment I didn't have to speak.

Geoff had never been a conventionally handsome boy, but he was nonetheless sexually attractive. I remembered him all through the long months of separation as I had known him that previous summer in Melbourne - bronzed and dashing in open necked shirts, tearing from meeting to meeting, relinquishing his numerous posts of office to younger, adoring disciples in preparation for his departure. Now before me on the wharf in Haifa bay stood a miserable dishevelled wreck of a man, swathed in a great army coat five sizes too big. His hair looked as if it hadn't been brushed since I last saw him, and he had the stubbly growth of an incipient beard. From the distance he looked like a hobo. I could not at that point even begin to imagine the conditions of life in Israel which had produced such a transformation. I was annoyed and hurt that he had made no effort to greet me, as I had him, in my Sunday best.

My long-anticipated entry into the Promised Land was no less of an anti-climax. By the time I had finished with the dozens of formalities on board, each requiring a twenty minute wait in as many different queues and being conducted in total chaos by incompetent petty officials, I forgot to kiss the soil at the bottom of the gangplank. Through eyes veiled with tears I saw fleeting images from our golden days and nights aboard the Neptunia: six passengers waited on by thirty stewards at dinner, serenaded by the ship's band under moon-lit tropical skies, entertaining each other with water ballets in the empty pool.

The passionate romantic reunion that I had visualized so many times fizzled to an embarrassed peck on the cheek. When I finally got close to him some six hours after docking, I realized too that he had a ghastly cold. There was a revolting clear drop of fluid on the end of his pointed nose which he hardly bothered to wipe away and when he did, reappeared within seconds.

Outwardly I carried on with all the spirit and enthusiasm with which my Zionist preparation had equipped me. But the contrast of the most magical and luxurious adventure of my young life with the harsh realities which I was now facing for the first time must have biased my perception of Israel from the outset. Indeed, 1951 turned out to be the worst year of physical hardship and deprivation in the entire history of modern Israel to date.

I had two heavy crates of luggage apart from the smaller stuff. I guess I was expecting a car, a taxi, maybe a kibbutz truck to appear. We stood there, on the wharf, chatting for some time and then walked in the direction of the Egged bus stop. Geoff had deposited the crates in bond in Haifa port to be collected at a later date and we lugged the rest with us. I was embarrassed even to ask what was happening and tried to divert conversation so that my disappointment would not show. We had grown worlds apart during the intervening year despite our regular exchange of letters. He had hardly mentioned the hardships of his life in Israel, perhaps not wanting to risk me changing my mind about coming. In any event, the reality now was that he was the seasoned Israeli and I the foreigner. What was perplexing me was not that I had expected some sort of transportation, but that Geoff knew that I would have expected it and yet we were both too embarrassed to discuss it. A sort of unspoken pact set in from the beginning: these were the conditions I was going to have to accept to win him, and accept without a murmur.

The bus journey to the kibbutz, like most else that was to happen that day, was memorable, not for the scenery nor my first impressions of the Holy Land that we had waited two thousand years to return to, but for the congestion, the shaking, the bickering, the muddy wet floor, the reckless driving and above all, the new chilling alienation and silent politicking which had replaced whatever else it was that Geoff and I had had going for us a year ago. There was little conversation by any of the passengers on the bus. Most people seemed to be exhausted. About an hour into the journey, without warning, the bus came to an abrupt halt. A policeman entered and ordered us all to leave the bus without taking any of our possessions. It seemed to be a familiar experience as there was no emotional reaction or resistance from any of the passengers. When we were all out of the bus three or four more policemen entered. Suddenly a cacophony of screaming chickens erupted inside the bus and again no reaction from the passengers assembled outside.

"Chickens bought or to be sold on the black market" Geoff explained "are on most buses. It's just a matter of chance which bus gets raided." The chickens were confiscated. I asked what would happen to them but nobody knew.

We changed buses in Afula, a small hick-town with a stinking urinal in the centre of the main street. This was my introduction to the sewage problems of the young State, but more on that later. I dealt with my immediate need to relieve myself by deciding to hang on till we reached the kibbutz.

The second bus ride was short, about twenty minutes. We were deposited alone in the middle of a deserted stretch of road and the bus drove off and disappeared. Night had fallen and before setting out on the last stretch of our journey on foot I took the longest, sweetest leak of my life, right there on the barren rocky terrain of the land of my ancestors. The relief was enormous. I was dirty and tired but suddenly re-spirited. We had arrived at our kibbutz, my new home. Silence and calm at last replaced the mighty storm of thirty hours before. We looked at each other, alone together for the first time in nearly a year and for a moment abandoned the new and unfamiliar shapes we saw in each other and hugged and hugged until it hurt; two lonely kids a million miles from home.

We gathered up the luggage and started climbing the winding dirt track that led to the kibbutz. Soon there would be light and food and warmth and people - my new home and my new family. There were about sixty souls in Kibbutz Barkai in 1951. The name means "morning star". It was a young kibbutz located almost in the centre of the country. It was composed mainly of young Americans, South Africans and Romanians, the latter being survivors of the Holocaust. The age range was from eighteen to thirty. There were also two sets of semi-retired parents, Rumanian of course, who had come with their children to live on the kibbutz and about ten babies born since its foundation. The kibbutz was a member of Kibbutz Artzi, belonging to Mapam, the left-wing socialist party of Israel. The system adopted was on the extreme left of socialist organization. All property was communally shared, all jobs on the kibbutz rotated, children lived apart from parents in children's homes etc. As far as possible no hired labour was to be employed. All major matters of policy were decided by the central committee of the Kibbutz Artzi movement.

The central committee of the Kibbutz Artzi movement was always a nebulous concept for me. I never knew where it was located nor who its members were. To me it was just Big Brother dictating what we ate, what we wore, what we read and what we thought. I came to hate it with an ever increasing ferocity. All decisions on matters specific to our kibbutz were decided by a majority vote of the kibbutz members at regular Saturday night meetings. We had practiced this in theory back on the training farm in Australia, but now I was about to experience it in reality.

We rounded the final bend in the tortuous path we had been climbing for the last ten minutes and suddenly there were people standing under a light in a clearing surrounded by several Nissen huts. A few passers-by noticed our arrival and nodded or smiled but did not stop to greet us. Geoff led me past the clearing and the Nissen huts which were located on the plateau on the top of the hill and we descended a hundred yards or so on the other side to a group of six small tents. We came to a halt outside one of them, put down our bags and Geoff expertly untied the ropes securing the entrance. The flap loosened and I caught my first glimpse of my new home:

two stretchers standing less than six inches off the bare soil, a hessian potato sack between them serving as a mat and a fruit box on its side between the heads of the two beds made a table.

On it was a bottle containing a few red and orange wild flowers beside a kerosene lamp. At the foot of one bed was Geoff's trunk. The bedroom I had left behind in my parents' home in Bellevue Hill flashed before my eyes with its pink wall-to-wall carpeting, matching drapes and bed- spread, the white lacquered furniture which my parents had bought me for my thirteenth birthday and the view of the cultivated flower- filled back garden.

Geoff was already stacking my luggage at the foot of the second bed and a string bag of red Italian apples I had brought with me off the ship was hung from a nail in one of the two supporting poles of the tent. I unpacked a clean change of clothes and armed with a neatly folded kibbutz towel, Geoff led me to the communal shower, the only concrete structure in the complex of communal buildings we had passed on our way in. It was divided into two sections, one for males and one for females. Inside it looked like the shower room of a large public swimming pool. Six shower roses along the far wall and the three remaining walls were flanked by a continuous bench, with evenly spaced clothing hooks above it.

How I came to love that shower room! It was to become blissfully connected with the end of a long hard day, with the soothing of tired, aching muscles, with billowing hot water in winter and cool relief in summer. It was the only cool place available to those of us who still lived in tents. We spent hours there after work in the long hot summer months to come. In retrospect it was a social centre, like the ancient Roman or Turkish baths - a Mediterranean institution.

After showering we made our way across the central clearing to the dining hut. That's all it was, a big ugly Nissen hut packed with rows of tables each seating six people. No chairs, just wooden benches. No attempt had been made to adorn it in any way. Each table was laid with an aluminium slop pan in the centre and a cutlery container with six knives, forks and spoons, six plates and a bowl of salt, a jug of water and six cups. People filled the tables consecutively as they entered and, as each table filled, the comrade on dining-room duty approached with a tray-mobile and unceremoniously dumped the carefully allocated portions of food on each plate with a soup ladle. As each table emptied, another comrade cleared it, wiped it down and re-laid it for the next round.

When Geoff and I reached the dining room most of the people had left and there were only a few latecomers. I followed Geoff to the table and by imitation tried as quickly as possible to slip into this silent ritual. A few people nodded to him, one or two even exchanged a sentence in Hebrew on the way in. We sat down, got through the unbelievably humble repast, emptied our slops into the slop pan and left. I was by now numb to all the emotional jolting. I had hardly registered what I had eaten or whom I had seen.

It felt good to be clean. The shower was the only ray of warmth in this whole miserable, unrelenting barrenness. Starkness seemed to characterize everything and everyone I had encountered since setting foot in Israel, Geoff included. He had taken on the austerity of the place, in his every action, thought and speech.

On the way back down to our tent he showed me the track leading to the toilets. Luckily, I did not need to face that encounter just then. Inside the tent Geoff busied himself lighting the *"petiliya"*, a primitive oil heater. I sat on my stretcher watching him and wondering what in the world might be appropriate to talk about. I groped for some bridge that might open a path between us, certainly nothing about my fairy tale trip. It would be bad taste in all this *"tzena"*, (*"tzena"*, I was soon to discover, was one of the most frequently used word in the Hebrew language in 1951. It meant "austerity"). Revelation of any of the emotions or impressions of my first day in Israel would be disastrous. I had by now had more than enough of the practical introductions to the workings of the kibbutz. I decided to ask about people, (his friends, if he had any). In the ideology of Kibbutz *Artzi* I knew that all the members are supposed to be brothers and sisters, one big happy family, but so far, no one had even acknowledged my presence. Geoff had not attempted to introduce me to anyone. Perhaps this, too, was laid down by the central committee of Kibbutz *Artzi* as the formal procedure for the introduction of a new member of the family.

We had not been in the tent five minutes when four young people appeared at the slit asking to come in. Their manner, and Geoff's in response, was suddenly transformed from anything I had encountered all that day. They were cheerful, colourful, light- hearted. Geoff untied the ropes to open the tent and invited them in. Geoff was acting host, offering them seats on our stretchers and making coffee on the *petiliya*. Not only was I introduced to them, but it was obvious that they had come specifically to meet me. They were American and South Africans, two couples, Geoff's special friends. I wanted to kiss them all. They were in technicolour. Everything else had been not even black and white, just a monotonous, damp grey.

We sat and talked and drank and smoked. The conversation went from kibbutz politics, to the American cigarettes I offered them. From time to time I noticed them eyeing the bag of red apples. I asked if anyone would like one and watched with vicarious pleasure as they devoured them. The conversation turned to food. I was soon to learn that food was a central topic in any social gathering. From juicy steaks in New York to pineapples in Cape Town, they seemed to supplement their meagre dinner with a diet of vivid imagery. But there were no complaints, no griping about the difficulties of life here. Furthermore, there seemed to be an assumed consensus that I had at last arrived at journey's end and attained the goal of my life-long ambition to escape the Diaspora. It seemed to be taken for granted that I was accordingly overjoyed to be home at last. They only stayed about an hour because on every day, apart from the sabbath, work started at 5 am.

They never became my special friends and, indeed, as the inevitable tensions developed, I dare say they became my enemies. Two of them I have forgotten entirely. They must have disengaged from Geoff soon after my arrival. The other couple, Moshe and Gila, remained close even as antagonisms grew. He was an extremely charismatic good-looking man in his mid-twenties; educated in a New York yeshiva (religious seminary), he spoke excellent Hebrew. He was the reigning head of the kibbutz and, as I was to learn later, he was grooming Geoff to be the next one. Election to this post was, as with everything, by majority vote of the kibbutz members. But this position needed special training, so there was usually only one candidate at a time available to stand for election. Gila, Moshe's roommate and future wife, was an incredibly hard working, super idealistic woman; she oozed discipline. She could hold her own with any male in the fields and was already developing the appearance of a muscular peasant woman. When I saw her again ten years later, she was so leathered by the sun that she looked like a woman of sixty.

We rose at 4:45 the next morning. It was pitch dark. Geoff fumbled for the oil lamp. It was also very cold and damp. Outside it was raining again. Geoff dressed in his work clothes and I realized that he **had** been in his Sunday best yesterday. Everything was always too big for him. He was one of the tallest men on the kibbutz and thin at the best of times. He had lost a stone since coming here. The acute lack of protein and sugar in the diet affected most of the men in this way, while the women gained weight. The aesthetic results were unfortunate.

Geoff left for work in the tobacco fields and I was to spend the day exploring the kibbutz for myself. I rummaged in my bags for the warmest clothes I could find. My gumboots were still in Haifa and outside the tents the paths were slushy with mud. I made my way to the shower room and again there was no one there. I soon discovered why; no hot water in the mornings! I washed minimally and descended to the fork in the dirt paths leading to the toilets.

There I found a small queue. I smiled an embarrassed smile and decided to return later. The uncouthness of it all. If I had to overcome shitting into a hole in the ground, I didn't need someone outside the flimsy tin hut listening to me "kvetching" as well. We had not been prepared for this aspect of Kibbutz life in the training farm at Shepparton.

Finally when I could no longer stand the pressure on my bladder and with no one in sight for a hundred metres in all directions, I made my assault, slowly pushing against the wooden door. It would not open. Someone must be inside! I fled, half happy at yet another reprieve, but by now my need was becoming desperate. Before my eyes stood the little 10-year-old girl in line to the teacher's desk at Kambala and I suddenly remembered that that too was in winter and it was cold. But this time it was not the little Jewish girl who was about to wet her pants and make a puddle on their clean Christian floor, but the Australian Jewish princess spoilt rotten by degenerate Diaspora capitalism. I marched resolutely back up the hill, yanked on the door of the second tin hut and found it opened out, not in - there was no one there at all!

With eyes closed tight, I pulled my pants down, squinted just sufficiently to see where the hole was, squatted and peed. It was a long, long pee, seemingly hours. Slowly my pulse rate abated and the sound of my urine hitting the squelchy bottom of the pit came into focus. It seemed much deeper than I had expected. I opened my eyes and let go my breath. It was pitch black within the hut. The stench was indescribable. I held on without taking another breath for several seconds. I pulled my pants up, pushed open the door and turned to glance, just once, down into the hole - it was one huge solid mass of crawling bugs, bright gold in colour, writhing and coiling like a pit of snakes!

I returned to the tent to finish dressing. It was too dismal, too dark and cold to stay there alone. Even though I wasn't yet hungry enough to eat, I decided to try the dining hall. The concrete floor was covered in puddles of muddy water. I marched in and sat down at the first unfilled table. A girl at the table spoke to me:

"You must be Geoff's *bachura* (female partner). I am Chani" she said, in a slightly European accented American English.

"I am Helen, pleased to meet you."

She only drank the tea and smoked a cigarette and I decided to join her. The tea had the same sickly chemical taste I had noticed in the coffee the previous evening.

There was apparently no sugar at all available for adults in the kibbutz. What meagre supplies we received or bought on the black market were for the children and pregnant women. Chani worked in the children's kitchen and invited me to come to see her there later in the morning. She left in a hurry.

I stayed, spinning out the cold, sickly-sweet saccharinated tea and looked around me. Everyone was in a hurry. Breakfast consisted of spring onions, a hard-boiled egg, sour milk and large lumps of black bread and of course the tea. There was no butter. Sometimes there would be margarine, *"bemanot"*! *"Bemanot"* was another early word to learn in 1951. It means in allocated portions (rationed) as opposed to *"beoffen hofshi"*, freely available (unrationed). Most people, unlike Chani, were eating heartily. Some made big jumbo sandwiches out of their eggs and bread and took them off to work. No-one talked, some of them seemed half asleep. Outside a small truck was honking hysterically for its passengers. Within twenty minutes the hall was almost empty.

One of the guys on kitchen duty came to clear our table. He smiled and said *"Shalom"*. Once the rush was over, inter-human relations seemed to return. I was already recognizing this to be a special convention of the kibbutz. One did not bother with human discourse while doing anything else. That's how Geoff had been yesterday; that's how everyone was, unsmiling, serious, remote, while doing anything other than being social. They seemed to compartmentalize their behaviour.

I looked into the kitchen, attached to the dining room. It was like any canteen kitchen with the minimum of mass cookery equipment: a bread slicer, which took a loaf at a time, two huge cooking cauldrons and two large double sinks. One guy standing there, hands red raw from the cold water, was washing mountains of plates. Everyone in the kitchen wore gum boots and the slosh on the stone floor was patterned with the designs of the soles of their shoes.

I felt a weary resignation in the comrades to the tough conditions. A few seemed able to rise above them, usually those in positions of some authority, plus a couple of divinely inspired, indomitable spirits that inevitably surface in any group under stress. The material conditions were tough; tougher than they had ever been since the inception of the State four years earlier and tougher than they have ever been since. But I think that it would have been better for us all if some effort had been made to retain something of the inessential trivia of life. It was as though the last drop of energy was expended in just meeting the bare essentials necessary for survival and there was nothing left over for anything else. One can push the boundaries in times of acute emergency such as wars or catastrophes, but not in a situation of relative permanence. It occurred to me that the Englishman who dressed for dinner in the wilds of Africa may, after all, not have been mad but affirming to himself that he was never extended beyond his capability to cope.

I made my way out of the dining room and stood for a while surveying the kibbutz in the first light of dawn. The hill on which it stood, like most of Israel at that time, was cruelly barren ; not a single established tree as far as the eye could see. The only greenery was the tiny saplings that the two older retired couples had planted outside their pre-fab huts and down in the valley the rows of small banana plants and other agricultural enterprises of the kibbutz.

The main service huts were situated in a circle on the next level down the hill from the dining hall and shower rooms. Then followed our six tents, the semi-permanent prefabricated houses and finally the cow sheds, chicken pens and tobacco sorting rooms. Our kibbutz grew tobacco and was planning at that stage to develop it as a special industry.

I started my tour with the *"machsan"* (storeroom). Inside the walls were lined with shelves of neatly stacked clothes. Two women were busily sorting and folding enormous piles of unironed clothing. A radio was playing classical music. Next came the laundry, sensibly situated close by. Again two women were busily sorting piles of dirty clothing. Here there was rudimentary equipment: a huge commercial washing machine and a tailor's steam iron, plus the vestiges of what must have been the original laundry, a coal-fired copper and double-troughs. Again, a radio was playing the same classical music. As I moved from centre to centre and finally down to the extremities of the kibbutz, I heard the same music everywhere, probably selected by the Central Committee of Kibbutz Artzi dignifying the menial labours of this new proletarian intelligentsia

In the children's house I sensed this same soul-destroying regimentation, which again I imagine must have come directly from the Central Committee. Each child's corner featured a different basic colour but was identically equipped. I sensed that the worst of all the latest philosophies of child-rearing were being practiced here. There was a predetermined way of talking to the children, of eating, sleeping and playing. It had all been formulated and then circulated by the Central Committee. In those days I had little knowledge of and even less interest in these ideological questions. But my first encounters with the workings of Zionist socialism sent me reeling in the opposite direction.

During my first six months in the kibbutz I worked my way through every job, from kitchen duty to sorting tobacco and found nothing I liked. Finally, I was given a plum job in an experimental laboratory attached to a food factory some seven kilometres from the kibbutz. The factory was jointly owned by several kibbutzim, but there was no special committee determining policies on how to run factories owned by the kibbutzim as they were still a rarity. The head of our laboratory was a mad German Jewish professor. He was probably a genius who had survived the Holocaust. I never got to know anything about him, except that he was quite crazy. We made the most incredible concoctions out of corn. Our task was to produce as many products as we could out of the corn seed, with the help of a few available chemicals. We made baby puddings, a meat flavouring for vegetables, an ersatz honey and a kind of barley-water drink. The chaotic turbulence of our lab run by a mad professor and the mere fact of getting out of the confines of the kibbutz each day lifted my spirits. On my day off, I would smear my lips with lipstick, which was against

Kibbutz Artzi policy and which I had hardly ever worn in Australia, and hitch a ride to Tel Aviv

My horror of all this socialist regimentation reached its zenith with the Chani-Skate affair. Skate was Chani's South African fiancé. They had met at Barkai a couple of years earlier and some months prior to my arrival Skate had returned to South Africa, to finalize his affairs before immigrating permanently to Israel. Five months later, a letter had arrived saying that his return to Barkai was delayed by unforeseen complications and he wanted Chani to join him in South Africa for the moment. He enclosed the money to cover her fare.

Chani, being a member of the kibbutz, needed its permission to go. The matter would, of course, have to be decided by vote at the forthcoming Saturday night members' meeting. The issue was discussed incessantly during the preceding days. The suspicion was that Skate was not intending to return at all. Chani needed the kibbutz's permission to go in order to leave open her option to return. She was a war orphan with no other ties in the whole world. The kibbutz was her only home and to leave without its members approval would have deprived her of the right of ever returning.

The matter was duly discussed at the Saturday evening meeting and put to the vote. Her friends voted for her to go, about a dozen people in all. Everyone else was against. The issue was not decided on the strength of any arguments, either practical, humanitarian or ideological, but on personal prejudice. Jealousy was not a small factor amongst those who had no opportunities for travelling outside the country and was even raised as a reason against granting her permission. The motion was defeated. Chani abided by the majority decision and never saw her fiancé again. Skate was killed in a motor car accident one month later.

Apart from providing a home for Holocaust survivors, the kibbutzim were also responsible for defending Israel's borders, feeding the population and establishing an agricultural base in the country. In all four capacities they were eminently successful. They produced thousands of hard-working, dedicated and honest people who fought and struggled nobly to build and defend Israel. Two of the political giants of Israel's first twenty years, Ben Gurion and Golda Meir, never ceased to laud the virtues and valour of the kibbutzniks. They contributed more proportionately to the redemption of the land and its defence than any other sector of society. The fanatical ideology associated with the kibbutz movement served a practical purpose in the extremely tough conditions of those early days but as the kibbutzim have now long ceased to fulfil these pioneering functions, it has accordingly withered .

Within six months a monumental struggle for Geoff, between me and the kibbutz had begun. It was obvious that I was not going to spend the rest of my life on a kibbutz, but they really wanted to keep Geoff. The issue of whether a couple should split up when one wants to leave the kibbutz or whether they should both leave together was tabled for reference to the Central Committee

In our halcyon Habonim days in Australia we used to dance the hora round the campfire singing our own adaptation of a famous Al Jolson song which began with the words "San Francisco here I come" :

"Israel, Israel, here we come
Right back where we started from.
Australia, Australia, to you we sing,
Of races, dance places,
football, pictures, everything.
But we don't want your life of ease.
We'll have our own country please.
So open up, open up, open up, those
pearly gates,
Israel, here we come!"

Oh my God! How stupid, how naive we were! I had marched fearlessly into my new life with Geoff, but from its very beginning I began building a resistance to Israel and everything in her. Israel was no longer even the unrelieved grey of that dismal November day which had blanketed my arrival in Haifa in such gloom. She had become a prison, with everything good outside and everything bad inside: an echo of my childhood perception of Jewish darkness versus Christian sunshine

Maybe the whole Jewish saga--the plagues on Egypt, the forty years in the desert, the Chosen People bit, the two-thousand years in the wilderness, even the realisation now of the "next year in Jerusalem" mantra, had simply been our myths. Every nation has its mythology. But English kids don't go looking for the Holy Grail after learning about their King Arthur and his knights. Only I had to keep digging and stirring until all my myths blew up in my face. I had bitten into a shiny red apple in my Garden of Eden and choked on a mouthful of worms.

With each new experience in Israel, I felt more and more alienated from my Jewish heritage. I wanted to escape. I wanted out! But before I could make the final break, I had first to go through the motions of proving to Geoff that staying in Israel outside the kibbutz was impossible. Then I would face the far greater challenge of reassembling my shattered image of myself.

CHAPTER 8

YERIDA* (The Descent)

We left the kibbutz in May 1952 and made for the city. Geoff got a job with the Jerusalem Post which had just one year earlier replaced the Palestine Post, Palestine's only daily English newspaper since 1932.

We found a room to let in a private flat with a Mrs Granitmann, a remarkable lady of seventy. There seemed to be goods in the shops of sorts, but few people had the money to buy them. Breakfast, lunch and dinner for Mrs Granitmann consisted of diluted saccharinated

---

Yerida*: **emigration from Israel (literally to descend.)

tea, dry bread and jam. She never complained. She had been born in Palestine of immigrant parents from Russia. She entertained us with glowing tales of adventure and plenty in the days of the Mandate and of course, her youth. She spoke to me in an atrocious Yiddish.

Her standard was on a par with mine, learnt in much the same circumstances by listening to her elders as a child.

My most vivid recollection of Israel in the fifties is the relentless glare of sunlight. The whole country, including the cities, was shade less - white sand and stone. There was hardly a grown tree in the land and there are seven cloudless months in Israel, from May to November.

Life in the towns was even grimmer for most people than on the kibbutz. There at least the economic worries were shared. City people were harried, nervous, unsmiling. Many were carrying unbearable memories of horrors, at that time still unspoken and unspeakable. It was often difficult to gauge a person's age. Most people looked worn out. On the streets I often thought that I could be passing members of my own family; women who resembled my aunts, men who looked like uncles and children who could have been my little cousins, now ashes and dust.

One day while we were sitting in a sidewalk cafe in Tel Aviv, a grey- haired woman with that tell-tale hollow look of Holocaust survivors in her eyes approached us with a slim leather case. She had an air of vanished aristocracy. She sat down and with hands trembling uncontrollably, fumbled to unlock the case. Inside was a collection of shoelaces, matches, hairpins, brooches, new and old, mixed in a higgledy-piggledy mess. I looked closer into her face; she had the high Tartar cheekbones and the blue-green eyes of my mother. I gently placed an American dollar note amongst the junk on her tray and she started to weep hysterically. After regaining her composure, she put the dollar back in my hand and again offered us her wares to choose from. With hands now trembling like hers, I selected a few pieces and again handed her the dollar, which she now accepted and stuffed into the cleft between her breasts. She relocked the case, got up and left without a word.

In Tel Aviv I visited a distant cousin of my mother's. He and his wife had survived the war, but not their nineteen-year-old daughter. After the war they had adopted the orphaned child of some dead friend. In two rooms of the apartment all was sunny and bright; the husband joked and played incessantly with their adopted child. But the third room was kept in darkness with a burning candle in front of the dead girl's photo.

Nothing seemed to reach the city without the intervention of the black marketeers. Onions we had grown in the kibbutz and sold for eight agorot a kilo were nowhere to be found for less than eighty in the shops. One of the few foods in the whole country containing real sugar was black market chocolate. We ate a block each day and I put on weight till I could hardly fit into my clothes.

The flat hunting was leading nowhere. We couldn't find an apartment for less than Geoff's entire salary at the Jerusalem Post and I couldn't find a job at all. I had only completed one year of a university science course at Sydney University and I had next to no Hebrew, having successfully resisted all attempts to teach me anything on the kibbutz. We floated for a month or so till Geoff agreed with me that we must return to Australia where I would complete my degree and he would earn and save money and one day we would return…maybe.

The cheapest and quickest way home was on an Italian ship. In order to get a double berth on an Italian Catholic ship we had to present a marriage certificate, so we set about getting married in Israel. Israel was and still is to this day, a semi-theocratic state: birth, death and marriage are in the hands of the Rabbinate. By Rabbinical law the banns had to be published one month in advance of the wedding ceremony. But there were only three weeks left before the counting of the Omer, the period in which no marriages can be celebrated. We would have to wait till after that. But our endurance was running out and so was our money, so although it would be more expensive, we decided to travel in separate berths. But on a last visit to Barkai to say our farewells we were given a reprieve. The kibbutz had a rabbi who was blind but endowed by the Almighty only to see money. He would come twice a year to the kibbutz to perform mass marriages, needed in order to obtain the extra food rationing coupons issued to married couples. (Why married couples should merit extra food rations I cannot imagine). We were told where to go to bribe our way through the rabbinical bureaucracy in Tel Aviv to speed up the printing of the banns and then return to Barkai where their private rabbi would be summoned to marry us.

The next day we found ourselves facing a bearded, black robed mediaeval Jew. I don't know if he was a rabbi or not, they all looked the same to my untrained eye. After explaining the difficulties of printing the banns at this time of the year, he produced a Jewish National Fund blue box from the drawer in his desk, unceremoniously lifted off the normally welded lid and sat staring straight at us. Geoff put in an American dollar note. "Not enough" he protested. In went another and another, until we reached twenty. The lid was replaced, and our details taken: names, age and addresses, separate of course, and parents' names. Rachel and Abraham were fine, I passed, but Alec and Marie turned all hell loose. Marie was not a Jewish name. In fact, it was a very Christian name. We would have to produce proof that Geoff was a Jew. We claimed it was a mistake, it should have been Miriam. We tried another five dollars, to no avail. We had to get a statement certified by a rabbi that Marie was a Jewess. We argued and bargained and settled at last for a telegram from the Melbourne Synagogue.

Meanwhile, the kibbutz rabbi agreed to publish our hard-earned banns and withdraw them if the telegram was not forthcoming. Communication systems in Israel were in a state of chaos. The Jews had excelled in many fields in their long sojourn in the Diaspora, but all the indications are that not one had ever worked in a post-office. For ten years after we left Israel my anxiety dreams were always about telephones; either my fingers would go limp so I couldn't dial past the first couple of digits, or if by some superhuman effort I got through the dialling, the receiver would melt in my hand. But sending the telegram proved surprisingly easy. Apart from the usual chaos at the post office (just entering an Israeli bureaucratic office sends my blood pressure up, even today) it was a straightforward procedure, much simpler than a long-distance call. And having accomplished it we returned to the kibbutz to proceed with arrangements for the wedding.

Next came a visit to the kibbutz rabbi's house. This was located in a small house in Pardes Chana, a gorgeous little rustic village about five miles from Barkai. The Rabbi had already been informed of our problem and was well prepared for the impending bargaining session. His price was ten dollars for him and twenty dollars towards the building of the new mikveh (ritual bath). Dates were set for my mandatory prenuptial *mikveh (ritual bath)* and the wedding itself. We were going to get our money's worth! When we returned for the ceremony, we were to bring the printed banns with us along with the certificate from the mikveh. Suddenly it dawned on us that we need not have bothered with the telegram after all, because the whole enterprise had become possible only because this Rabbi was blind to everything other than money. He hadn't even asked who our parents were, let alone requiring us to prove that they were Jewish.

A day before the wedding I had to go to the local mikveh which comprised a stone hut with a deep concreted hole in the ground about four- foot square, by six foot deep. I was met and welcomed by a filthy, toothless old hag who enfolded me in her voluminous rags, embraced me and started to lecture me in a Levantine Hebrew which I had never heard before. She enhanced the lecture with copious gesticulations and I gathered that amongst other things, she had worked very hard to clean the mikveh well for the American tourist and that I was to strip. She approached me with a non-too clean comb, missing as many teeth as herself and proceeded to comb my hair, head and crotch! I was led to the bath and descended an iron side-ladder into it. She pushed me down under water and I reflexively raised one arm to hold on to the edge. She was screaming hysterically at me to let go and pushing me under, again and again. She finally grabbed my hand and pushed it in too and I realized that some hocus pocus demanded that I be fully submerged. This, it turned out, had to happen not once but three times. My stomach and ears were filled with water by the time I emerged, looking like a drowned cat. She dried me maternally and was, I think, instructing me in the joys of the nuptial bed. From the glint in her eyes, she was not telling me to lie back and think of the Empire. Outside she wanted payment and whatever it was that Geoff gave her was, of course, not enough for such an extra special job for the American tourist. We were used to it by now.

The wedding was set for the next day. We arrived at the rabbi's house at 2 pm. On the doorstep a man of about seventy was beating his breast and wailing. He was on a hunger strike because the rabbi would not give him a divorce from his wife who would not follow him to Israel from Iraq. Incidentally, refusing to follow one's spouse to the Holyland is a specifically prescribed reason in the Talmud* for granting a Jewish divorce. The agreed price had, no doubt, not yet been reached. In the backyard a primitive *chupah* (bridal canopy) had been erected. Chickens were running about under it, scratching in the dirt. The rabbi, dressed in full regalia, stepped over the prostrate old man on a hunger strike and called us to assemble. We had brought two witnesses with us from Barkai. A throng of neighbours and children, some without pants had arrived to join the festivities.

The age-old ceremony was much as I had seen it on several occasions before in the style and pomp of the Great Synagogue in Sydney. But we seemed to be drinking a great deal more sips of the sweet red wine for blessings and I had to dance seven times around the groom, followed in high spirits by the pantless kids clapping in rhythm to some Chassidic melody. Everyone was getting high on the half percent grape juice. We

*Talmud: book of the Jewish oral law.

danced our way into the house to collect the prized certificate, shook hands all around and left on foot, down the dirt track that led back to the main road to Tel Aviv, Rome and home wherever that might now be?

CHAPTER 9

THE WILDERNESS YEARS

Getting out of Israel was like returning to civilization. To my delight there was enough to spare, over and above the sheer necessities of life. It showed in everything. People had time to spare, thought to spare, comfort to spare. There were soap and towels in public washrooms, paper in public toilets, sugar bowls on cafe tables, spare seats in trains and buses. Furniture was sprung, floors were carpeted, trees gave shade. I was aware of details of life that I had never before noticed: the civility, the calm, the quiet, the comfort. How glad I was to have escaped!

But I knew it was not a clean cut. I knew already then, in the midst of all the exaggerated passion and revulsion at the shock that Israel had been, that I could not excise her from my soul by just leaving, any more than the Holocaust had been cut out of our lives by not talking about it. At that moment, though, all I wanted was to be shot of her. I had no inkling then that I would have lived in four different continents and be one quarter of a century older before I would again try to come to grips with her.

Once back in Australia. Geoff and I set about restoring some normality to our disrupted lives. Geoff entered his father's law practice in Melbourne, I went back to University, this time in Melbourne to finish my science degree . Our parents, thrilled with our return to the straight and narrow, helped in every way they could. Within four years we had a lovely apartment, a car, a science degree, a partnership in the law firm and a couple of bouncing babies,

We mixed freely with all people outside home, at the law firm and at University. But inevitably the old pattern re-emerged. Those with whom we came to feel comfortable were usually Jews.

On our return to Australia, Geoff had announced dogmatically that he would never return to Israel and that he would never again make promises such as he had made to me, that he would leave Israel if I did not want to stay. I did not take him seriously at the time. I thought it was more a manifestation of his anger with me for having ruined his plans and that he was telling me that I would not be able to salve my conscience by rationalising that we would return to Israel sometime in the future. I had enormous confidence in his good sense and so I also assumed that part of the message was that we must relinquish our hopes of returning in order to devote ourselves properly to our future in Australia. He presented an exterior of absolute confidence in his decisions. He believed that the solution to the Jewish problem was either for all the Jews in the world to go to Israel or, for those who did not to disappear via assimilation into their host societies.

The threat (or punishment) in his pronouncement fell on deaf ears. I did not really care what was going to happen in the far distant future. He did not try to impose the second part of his formula for the solution of the Jewish problem upon me but slipped docilely into the Jewish social set that we eventually gathered around us.

But he never again evinced the slightest interest in Israel and in his second marriage he had indeed pursued the path of assimilation into Australian Gentile society. During the remaining thirteen years of my marriage to him I did not question his total disinterest in Israel. I was rather relieved that he had had the good sense not to sour our relationship with recriminations for my having sabotaged his plans. But in retrospect I have often wondered how he managed so completely to relinquish the Zionism of his youth. Perhaps the explanation lay in his personality. He was an extremely intellectual but unemotional person. His alternatives for the future of the Jewish people must have been equally acceptable to him. What then caused him to choose the Zionist solution in the first place? The conclusion I arrived at, years later, was that Geoff saw the Jewish question and its solution as a personal problem. Having been obstructed in his ambition to make a career for himself in the Australian Diplomatic Service, he had simply moved his political ambitions to Israel*. Perhaps it was this very obstruction that had brought him to his analysis of the Jewish destiny. Once he had again been frustrated in achieving his personal ambitions in Israel because of me, he quite naturally accepted the alternative path to assimilation.

I lived with Geoff in Australia in blissful suburbia, raising our kids and entertaining our Jewish friends till 1965. My marriage to Geoff built on such tenuous foundations predictably just drifted into nothingness. Our only hope may have been to have found some other joint ambition to replace our failed Zionism, but nothing ever happened. We slipped comfortably into predestined

---

*Jews were excluded from serving in the Australian Diplomatic Service at that time, whether officially or not, I do not know but they were certainly barred in practice just as they were also barred from the stock exchange and many social clubs

roles in our society. What we had in common at nineteen was an extraordinarily high motivation to change course. After Israel we never found and never really sought another.

CHAPTER 10

JUDAISM TRANSCENDED

Geoff and I drifted further and further apart emotionally. Inevitably one of us found another person with whom to fill the void. It happened to be me first.

I fell hopelessly in love with a young Jewish doctor, the father of three young children and as frustrated and bewildered by the sheer emptiness of his marriage, as I was of mine. It took us five years to convince ourselves that our situation was hopeless enough to warrant breaking up our families. By then too, the children were no longer quite so young and David and I escaped to try our luck at a second chance. He had left Australia with his wife and children in 1963 to do a post-graduate course in tropical medicine and demography at the London School of Hygiene and Tropical Medicine. He had gone in order to break our impossible deadlock, but it turned out to be the foundation of our new lives together.

When David left Australia, I returned to university to study for a further degree, this time in psychology and psychopathology. Sensing that my marriage to Geoff was doomed with or without David, I wanted a profession which would give me financial independence. Meanwhile, the separation between us, meant to finish the affair, served only to strengthen it, everything else in our marriages being just as wrong as before. In November 1965 I flew to join David in Singapore where he had taken up a job financed by the British Foreign Office as family planning advisor to the Singapore government. I landed a plum job with the United Nations to design and conduct a study of the comparative resistances to acceptance of contraception amongst the three major ethnic groups (Chinese, Malay and Indian) in Singapore.

Our new careers in Population Control were to last for the next ten years and take us all over the world. The Jewish content of our lives inevitably receded in the context of our new interests. We were now dealing with a problem inextricably involving the entire human race. Furthermore, the adventure itself was so stimulating, so much was to happen to us that was new and exciting, that my interest in Judaism receded to what might be considered a more normal level.

We still sought out the Jewish communities in our new lands of residence and, more often than not, again found friendships amongst Jews. But our interests were diverted to other cultures, their joys and problems. We followed the fortunes of the young state of Israel with interest, if not passion, but began to feel ourselves more citizens of the world interacting as we were with other citizens of the world. Apart from Jews, Chinese and Indians, Swedes, Americans and Dutch people found their way into our personal lives.

The Jewish issue never arose in our interpersonal relationships even with Christian Chinese and Indians.

They were usually very devout Christians but the historical Judaeo-Christian conflicts seem insignificant or perhaps just unknown to these comparatively recent converts to Christianity. The "colour" issue superseded all other discriminations. We got on extremely well with most of the Chinese and Indians we met in Singapore and even became close friends with some of them. I felt more at ease with them than with Australians, no doubt because of this absence of anti-Semitism. Amazingly, we phobic Jews were able to cope more serenely with their colour sensitivities than our non-Jewish colleagues. We had extremely frank discussions about colour problems, probably because we were so dispassionate on these issues. While our Chinese and Indian friends saw us as "whites", unconsciously we did not and were always taken aback when they referred to us as such. We could empathize with them as fellow victims of discrimination.

The social problems which we did encounter stemmed from our ignorance of Oriental culture. We reacted by laughing them off. One of the most embarrassing was a Christmas party we organised for the staff associated with our work at the Kandang Kerbau Hospital, at that time the largest maternity hospital in the world. This was an investigation of the huge intra-uterine device (I.U.D.) family planning project jointly sponsored by the Singapore Government, the Population Council based in the United States and the British Department of Overseas Development. We had arranged a splendid ten course Chinese dinner-dance and invited the dozen odd nurses, young Chinese women aged between eighteen and twenty-three, to bring their boyfriends. A representative of the group informed us a few days later that they would not be bringing male escorts. Faux-pas number one! Chinese young women did not invite young men to accompany them anywhere.

Wondering how on earth we would entertain them without dancing, we decided to arrange some party games, amongst them a quiz competition. Before dinner we divided the young nurses into two teams and held our quiz competition. Everyone participated enthusiastically and all appeared to be going smashingly. Then, after the meal some two hours later and without forewarning, as soon as the last of the sumptuous traditional Chinese ten courses had been avidly devoured, the entire losing team rose from the table, thanked us politely for the party and left. The triumphant winning team stayed on till late into the night entertaining themselves magnificently without our help. We could not have been more offensive had we set out to design an evening to that end. We had created a situation in which one group inevitably had to lose face - the worst thing that can happen to a Chinese!

The colour sensitivity of Singaporean society even extended to the small Jewish community. References to skin colour in any context from serious political discussions to jokes were taboo. In the company of Singaporean Sephardi* Jews we were suddenly more aware of ourselves as white than Jewish.

*Sephardi Jews: Oriental Jews as opposed to Ashkenazi Jews who live in the Western world. Sephardi Jews in general have darker skins than Ashkenazi Jews.

This was a social barrier which took years of effort to overcome and only receded in friendships we retained after leaving Singapore. As far as I was concerned, this barrier was created wholly by them. I did and still do feel at one with the whole of the Jewish people. Certainly, we encountered what were to us bizarre differences due to the intervening centuries of separate cultural influences, such as the array of decrepit seventy-year-old Jews with their multiple young Chinese brides on display on Friday nights up in the women's gallery of the local synagogue.

But I found more in common with these Oriental Jews than anything which divided us, as I do still do today with the Sephardim (Oriental Jews) in Israel. Notwithstanding all our cultural and genetic divergences our religious purity seemed unblemished. We were as united in common traditions on the Jewish high holydays as we might have been, had the Romans never conquered ancient Israel and dispersed us to the ends of the earth.

To celebrate Passover and Jewish New Year the whole of the tiny Jewish community would assemble each year in the celebrated home of the late Mrs. Nissim. This eighty-year old woman was a legend in her time. On the high holy days all ex-patriate Jews in Singapore had a seat at her table. Until the time of her death in 1975 her beautiful colonial mansion was a sort of Jewish communal centre in Singapore. In her last years, too frail to participate, she would appear for a few moments to greet her guests, leaning on the shoulder of her childhood Chinese amah, now a little gnarled walking stick of ninety-five.

During our time in Singapore, the 1967 war broke out in Israel, and we were treated to an inmate view of Israel's centrality and importance to world Jewry. This tiny community of less than five hundred families was thrown into uproar.

The head of the community and ex-prime minister of Singapore, David Marshall, a Sephardi Jew of Baghdadi descent opposed any public support for Israel at that moment. Surrounded by Muslim countries and with some twenty percent of Moslems within the Singapore population itself, he feared the consequences of such a demonstration. The community opposed him to a man. A collection was taken up and prominent members of the community volunteered their services via the newly established Israeli consulate. There was a rush on shortwave radios and the little community held its breadth and then exploded in joy as Israel fought and triumphed.

But Singaporean Jewry was also a dying community. The young people were encouraged by their parents to leave, despite the flourishing economic situation, to find Jewish marriage partners in larger communities. With the enormous exodus of Oriental Jewry from Muslim lands after the establishment of modern Israel and the disintegration of these Jewish outposts even in non-Muslim countries of Asia such as in Singapore and Hong Kong, we may be witnessing the demise of Jewry in Asia after a sojourn of thousands of years.

We completed our stay in Singapore, mission successful, in May 1968. The overcrowded wards of the huge maternity section in the K.K. hospital were already beginning to thin. When we had arrived there in 1965 women were accommodated two to a single bed. They were placed head to toe in opposite directions for a short recovery period after childbirth. On bad days mattresses were placed under beds on the floor and women lay there among the prodigious cat population that was encouraged in order to control the rat population. Singapore, situated close to the equator, is hot in winter and hotter in summer and in the 1960's, air-conditioning was as yet a luxury. The wards of this enormous public hospital were stifling hot and pervaded with the stench of Chinese boiled fish which was, for some unknown reason, the food invariably offered to women after delivery. I never saw one patient eat it in the three years I worked there. Hundreds of stinking plates of bony fish were strewn over the floors for the cats and rats to devour.

When we returned to visit the hospital in 1972, it was like a ghost ship. Corridors once so crowded that we were unable to pass were now deserted; beds which had once each accommodated four women were now empty, despite the retraction of the maternity section to a tiny fraction of its original area. Order, cleanliness and smiling faces had replaced the tales of woe and hardship. Babies were wanted and treasured, instead of being the curse of yet another mouth to feed.

Singapore is one of the few success stories of population control. Its birth rate fell due to our family planning program from 45,000/year to 25,000/year in five years. As with "the one child policy" in China, this was the "sine qua non" for the transformation of Singapore from a third world to a first world country.

We completed our jobs in Singapore, in November 1968 and headed for London.

CHAPTER 11

TO LONDON VIA HELL

David had been appointed head of a new department in the British Foreign Office dedicated to population control and I had arranged to conduct a study on the psychological effects of vasectomy with the London School of Hygiene and Tropical Medicine

In June 1968 we flew from Singapore to London via Munich. This was the first time I had ever set foot in Germany and I was feeling nervous at the prospect. I started bristling with my first breaths of *Vaterland* air. As we passed through passport- control, the blond, blue-eyed Aryan official looked at the maiden name on my passport, Kuperszmit.

"Kuperszmit" he flashed a smile of recognition at me and purred "German?"

I have had five surnames and never felt comfortable with any of them. Three belong to my childhood, the other two to my husbands. None of the three childhood names ever came to mean the real me. They were used for separate purposes none of which was to identify my family, but to legitimise it in different situations. **Kuperszmit** was the name I found on my birth certificate when, at age 19 I applied for my first passport. Koupier was the name my mother had coined to promote herself as French. Madam Koupier became a leading interior decorator for the Australia aristocracy. But neither my mother nor her aristocratic clients were aware that there is no letter "K" in the French language! Cooper was the way Australians pronounced Koupier unless corrected. At school I always felt that my name was used like the mark of Cain, to single me out for something. I hated the approach to my spot on the roll- call. The teachers always stumbled on it: "KOUPIER" in 3 thundering syllables- Kou...pi...er. The children would use it a as a weapon against me in fights - Helen KOO-PI-ER.

Now at last, I was about to have some joy from my name. Kuperszmit means coppersmith in German and the poor, innocent official took this to mean that I was an Australian of German background. He could not possibly have known what a hornet's nest he had stumbled upon.

"Kuperszmit, German?" the passport official repeated.

"No, Jewish" I answered sarcastically returning his friendly smile

The smile froze on his lips and I sailed past him, unexpectedly pleased with my entry into Federal Republic of West Germany.

We checked into a hotel and set out to experience our first evening on German soil. At six o'clock a man was hurled bodily through the glass wall of our hotel lobby.

He was cut and bleeding from his head. Glass was shattered all over the hall. No-one ran towards him nor away from him. Without emotion the hotel bell boys mechanically stacked the broken glass neatly in a corner. The ambulance arrived and removed the wounded man, and everyone went on drinking as though nothing had happened. I went out into the streets and caught my first glimpse of Munich night life - everyone, men, women and even children, drinking Munich beer. The whole city was warming up in one enormous swill. There were drunks singing and swaying together all over the place, while others were sparring and beginning to brawl as their blood alcohol levels rose.

In my imagination I was transported to the Nazi era of glory in this city. How did the Jews endure their fear in this drunken orgy when Hitler held power here? And then I remembered that many did not. I pretended that I was there, reliving the innermost thoughts of a Jew in Munich in 1938. I slunk into shadows as groups of inebriated Aryans passed me by. I planned escape routes in case I was attacked. I wondered how much false papers cost and how they could have worked in such a well-documented society. I noted the positions of sewer escapes in the streets and wondered if I would have had the courage to escape into them, even when running for my life. I remembered the story of a Jewish child caught in Hitler's nightmare, who said that he wished he could be a leaf on a tree.

On each of the three nights we stayed in Munich, people everywhere got drunk on the beer that literally flowed from taps all over the town. By morning the city had somehow miraculously sobered up and business resumed with relentless Teutonic efficiency. There was no way that I was going to enjoy my stay in Munich. I didn't want to see their monuments or their magnificent cathedral. The idea of making this a holiday was obscene. True twenty-three years had passed since the end of the war, but in 1968 at least half the people in the streets of Munich were alive in 1945. Just as God had allowed forty years in the wilderness to cleanse the Jews of their sins by allowing one generation to pass, it would still take another twenty years for me to overcome my rejection of the German nation.

Everything I did in those three days led me back to the Holocaust. Unfortunately, we had to eat. We settled for the ugliest restaurant in town - the Munich railway station. To our dismay the food was magnificent. The *brat-kartoffelen* and Bavarian cream lured us back. But as the gastric juices flowed, my mind retrieved my store of Holocaust food data : Zena, who almost drowned in a stampede into a barrel of pickled cucumbers which the SS deposited one day in Belsen concentration camp; the man who experienced the heights of joy each morning from the smell of a bakery on his way to work in a slave gang; pictures of Jewish children starving in the gutters of the besieged Warsaw ghetto; the Jewish woman whose breasts Dr Mengele ordered bound to see how many days her new born baby would survive without food; Paulette (aged three) who, with her sister (aged six) survived by stealing from farmyards in the French countryside; the soup made of human bones that the inmates of Auschwitz knew they were eating and yet ate.

Still I had to hand it to them after my trip to Munich - the Germans are superb cooks.

I wandered into a jewellery shop. There under one of the glass counters was a display of wedding rings. Wedding rings! All valuables were removed from those arriving at the camps, then sorted and documented. (Teeth and human fat were "humanely" delayed till after death). How many Jewish wedding rings had the Holocaust yielded the Third Reich? Six million Jews died, of whom one and a half million were children, two million men and two and a half million women. Let's say two million wedding rings (what's half a million here or there anyhow when talking of Jewish Holocaust victims). On each black velvet pad in the showcase of the Munich jewellery shop there were six rows of six rings; there were two shelves each with four pads. That made 288 rings in all. At that rate, 7,000 jewellery shops would be needed to display all the wedding rings of the Holocaust. But how many jewellery shops are there in Germany? I had no idea. And where were all these wedding rings now?

The question of German reparations to Israel was raging when I had spent my first year there in 1951. Like most issues in Israel the debate was passionate. Those in favour of accepting felt that Germany should at least be made to pay even though payment in money was meaningless. Those "against" felt that Israel must not give Germany the chance to absolve her guilt and regain respectability internationally through reparations to the Jewish people and therefore the Jewish State should have no dealings with Germany. Pragmatism prevailed and today thousands of Israelis travel in taxis all over the country behind the same Mercedes' emblem that adorned the engines of the trains that transported millions of Jews to the death camps.

My visit to Munich made me aware that the Holocaust had conditioned in me a gut revulsion to Germany and Germans. Most Jews that I know, even survivors of the Holocaust, can accept contact with young Germans who were born after 1945 or were still only children during World War II. But my intolerance of Germans was unqualified and beyond rational control. Whenever I saw happy German children, I also saw two little Jewish boys engrossed in a game with some pebbles on their way into the gas-chamber at Auschwitz and the German guard who halted the entire line to wait until they had finished their game before resuming the procession into the gas chamber. I did not blame German children for the Holocaust, I only rejected the right of their parents to their enjoyment of them. Under the circumstances I came to the conclusion that there are enough people in this world for me to do without Germans, guilty or not, and that they will have to resolve their guilt-complexes without my help. They seem to be managing admirably

CHAPTER 12

A CHILLING SILENCE

When we landed at Heathrow Airport in June 1968; the ground temperature was three degrees centigrade! It was a portent of what was to come during our three-year sojourn in England.

We took seven hours getting through customs. The British government at that time allowed its civil servants astronomical weight in accompanied baggage when returning from overseas assignments. We had dozens of cases and packages. Our transportation must have cost the British government several thousand pounds, but now every paltry item was being investigated for duty. The investigation was an inquisition, designed to catch us out on any false declaration. I was carrying an enormous fur coat which we had bought in Australia to allay my paranoid fear of the English winter. We had declared it truthfully as new on the customs form handed to us by the steward in the aeroplane. To our horror we were now being asked to pay more than its purchase price in duty. I explained that the coat was for my personal use only and I offered to sign an undertaking to export the coat when we left England, at the end of our tour of duties there. The answer was my first experience of the Brit's politics of envy:

"Why should you enjoy the duty-free use of a fur coat in England, when your neighbour cannot?"

We paid the duty into bond, with an undertaking on their part to give it back if I re-exported the coat within six months. We had to empty every one of the thirty odd boxes in our luggage, one by one. Suddenly in the midst of a pile of socks and underpants, one of our three inquisitors grabbed my wrist and demanded:

"Where did you get this watch?"

We declared the history of every knick-knack in our possession to the best of our ability and they made lists of manufacturers and identification numbers on our camera, tape recorder, radio and watches.

It was late at night when we finally sat exhausted on our cases on the pavement outside the arrivals hall. We had no hotel booking, a mistake we were never again to repeat in London. No matter when one arrived in London with its thousands of huge hotels in those days they were always booked out. The clerk at the airport hotel reservation counter searched the city hotels for vacancies and came up with the Savoy.

We hired two taxis and pulled up at midnight, filthy and dishevelled, me in jeans with my huge fur coat over my shoulders, in front of one of the poshest hotels in the world. A half dozen bellboys appeared within seconds to deal with our luggage. We were ushered in with the same pomp and ceremony accorded royalty. We were the objects of a set act and our appearance was irrelevant. They handled our string tied cardboard cartons as though they were a set of Gucci suitcases. Once into our room we realised that we would not have fitted into anything less than this unbelievably oversized Savoy Hotel bedroom originally designed for 19th century royalty.

The next morning, restored by a luxurious night's sleep, we set out to find more suitable temporary accommodation. By midday we had transferred our belongings to a serviced apartment in Hyde Park Square. From there we started the horrendous task of finding a suitable apartment to rent for our anticipated three year stay in England. The situation soon clarified itself: there simply was no honest rental accommodation to be had in London in 1968. The Government's policy of protecting tenants in the post-war shortage of rental accommodation against the greed of voracious landlords had resulted in the total elimination of all honest available unfurnished rental property. Instead there was a flourishing racket of key-money extortion, thinly disguised as the sale of furnishings, whereby rental accommodation was only available with the purchase of outrageously over- priced furnishings. We viewed dozens of apartments for which we would have had to pay to remove the junk furnishings for which we would have had to pay anything between five and ten thousand pounds.

In one last desperate effort to find something before throwing in the towel and telling the British government that either they had to provide accommodation for us or find someone else to open their new department for Population Control, I contacted one last real estate agent's office and coolly announced that we wanted a flat without any furniture; did they have one? To our amazement it was simply a case of "ask and ye shall be granted". We were shown a lovely Edwardian apartment on Moscow Road, Queensway in the process of being totally refurbished. It was owned by an enormous property company called the Freshwater Group, which owned thousands of apartments in London. All they wanted were respectable tenants who could be trusted to maintain their properties in good order. Our qualifications were apparently excellent. The rent of £40 per week being asked was extremely fair. We took the flat on the spot and immediately set about buying furniture and carpeting.

No sooner had we moved in than we received a delegation from our new neighbours. They welcomed us most cordially and offered all sorts of assistance with the local shopping and so forth. Soon they came to the serious business that had necessitated their contacting us so early. They virtually demanded that we should appeal to the rental tribunal against our outrageous rent! The flat must have been worth about eighty thousand pounds at the time, therefore our forty pounds a week rent represented a gross return of two and a half percent to the "voracious" landlord, out of which he was supplying us with free hot water, central heating, porterage and a lift! But the neighbours presented their side of the story: real estate values in London depended on capital appreciation, not rental returns and the correct going rent for our flat was twenty pounds a week because, according to the law, the landlord should only charge an incoming tenant the highest existing rental in the building, without reappraisal by the tribunal. If we honoured our contract without contesting it immediately, then forty pounds would automatically become the highest rental in our building and the beastly landlord might take them all to court to up their antiquated rents.

We felt uneasy about the morality of signing a contract and then contesting it. The neighbours insisted that this was standard practice and that the owners were expecting it. They would be aiming at achieving some increase on the existing rents but could not expect a hundred percent rise in one fell swoop. We were used to strange customs in new lands and "when in Rome", as the saying goes, "do as the Romans do". In any case why pay more if we could pay less, even for a bargain?

The tribunal was a farce. Everybody knew the outcome no matter what the evidence because of the prevailing political correctness of always favouring the underdog. We sat there covered in self-pity and sanctimonious righteousness at being screwed by the greedy landlord while awaiting his appearance. On the other side of a large desk sat the magistrate, a middle-aged gentleman immaculately turned out in a dark suit and shining black shoes. My husband (who was himself an Englishman) chatted with him, as one Englishman to another, about the weather and the cricket and whatever else Englishmen chat to each other about, when suddenly to our horror our landlord appeared - in the form of an orthodox Jew complete with skull- cap, black coat, beard and side-locks! It was unreal. There we were with Antonio and Portia, decrying the moneygrubbing rapacious Shylock!

We did not open our mouths throughout the entire proceedings. Nor did we need to. The poor Jew pleaded his case with resignation: how much he had improved the flat since the last tenant had vacated it; what services he was providing; the rise in city rates since the last tenancy, etc, etc. The magistrate, hearing not a word he said, waited with English civility till he had finished and peremptorily set the rent at twenty pounds per week! The Jew rose without a flicker of emotion on his face, thanked the court and "exited content".

Six years later the Freshwater Group of Companies collapsed. Antonio had had his pound of flesh and London lost its last surviving honest rental accommodation,

We were too new to the scene to assess what had really happened. I had been reared on the assumption of the inviolability of British justice. I had just witnessed a kangaroo court in action, of that I was sure. But whether British justice had been superseded by British envy or British anti-Semitism, or perhaps a bit of both, I had no idea. Looking back on this incident after our 3 years sojourn in England, I would give equal odds to both.

After the first week in our beautiful new apartment in Moscow Road, we cancelled our order at the local newsagent for the London Times. Its anti-Israeli bias upset us every morning. We soon found that we would have very little choice of newspapers. This was a very different situation from what we had been used to in Australia and in Singapore. After investigating we switched to the Telegraph, the only objective newspaper left in the country which I had always believed to be the world's most trustworthy source of information.

The BBC was just as bad. Soon after our arrival in England the Israelis bombed an Egyptian missile site. Rumours spread that it was not a missile site but a school, full of children. The BBC television news reported the incident faithfully, presenting both the Egyptian and Israeli conflicting reports and concluded with the item that a team of foreign journalists would inspect the site on the following day. But on the morrow I waited in vain for the report of the journalists' follow-up inspection. I rang the BBC immediately. With the greatest of British courtesy, I was given a lesson in British hypocrisy: I was told that the BBC deeply regretted any misrepresentation it may be guilty of by way of omission, but that was yesterday's news and only today's news is news.

I watched how the seeds of poison against Israel were being sown in England over the next three years. We wrestled incessantly with this bias with whatever humble means we had, to no avail. Not one of our letters to various editors was ever published. We confronted Jews who worked in the media only to be told that they would lose their jobs if they raised their voices in protest.

The anti-Israeli stance of the British media was evident from the day we arrived. The anti-Semitic underlay took a little longer to discern. Every now and then, out of the blue there would appear some totally irrelevant, blatantly anti-Semitic article, like the one about a Mrs. Rosenberg in a Sunday Times magazine in 1968, who had underpaid her maid back in 1926; or the evergreen, notorious adventures of the odious Mr. Rachman, the archetypical greedy landlord, with an unfortunately unmistakable Jewish name. These blatantly anti-Semitic articles appeared to be pulled out of some reservoir for no other purpose than to simply fill space when real news was scarce. What shocked me even more was the total absence of objection to such blatant anti-Semitism by British Jews or anyone else.

With the arrival of Easter, I encountered my first personal experience of overt anti-Semitism in England. Even though we were non-observant Jews we had matzos (unleavened bread) in the house at Passover because we liked them. I had by then been working at the London School of Hygiene and Tropical Medicine for four months. I used to eat lunch daily with a non-Jewish colleague in the cafeteria. She had befriended me, rather than I her and she would come to collect me from my office at one o'clock each day. Suddenly after the first appearance of my matzos she stopped coming. After a couple of days, I went to find her. She was busy for lunch today, working tomorrow, shopping the next day. I asked a mutual friend to find out if I had offended her in any way. No, there was nothing wrong. I confronted her face-to-face with my suspicions and I drew a blank. This, I concluded, was the stuff of real British anti-Semitism - **a chilling silence.**

This incident enraged me, almost beyond self-control. I wanted to punch and scratch and scream, but there was nothing to hit. If I had been hypersensitive to anti-Semitism before I was now fast becoming super hypersensitive. I embarked upon a crusade of exposing British society for what I now felt it to be; a festering cesspool of anti-Semitism.

We picked away at every scab until the pus shot forth. David and I were invited to a dinner party to celebrate the publication of the host's first book on the world population problem. The author came from the ranks of the landed gentry and had inherited a minor title. He was born in colonial India during his father's tour of duty there. This was, I guessed, the lower echelons of the British aristocracy. There were about twenty guests and the evening was swinging along beautifully with everyone getting slightly inebriated as was expected of them. I understood little of the clever banter passing to and fro around me, but David was in his element. Suddenly I heard someone say,

"I'm really a Turk" in the best Oxford accent,

"Well I'm an Indian" responded the host

"And I'm a Jew" my husband proclaimed, a little too loudly.

The whole room came to a sudden halt, like a stuck movie reel. After several silent seconds' recovery time, our host stammered,

"So is my wife... that is... I mean, my wife's a Catholic,"

There must be some common denominator between the rejection of Jews and Catholics, I imagined, to provoke this Freudian error.

"Anyway, I don't mind" he continued compounding the awkwardness of the moment.

Slowly little groups of hushed conversations resumed around the room. But the party was over. It was now obvious that we'd never have been invited had they known we were Jewish. Most of the guests soon left deliberately ignoring our presence. To the consternation of our hosts we stayed on stoically to the bitter end.

There was, of course, a great deal more happening to us in London than this tunnel vision of British anti-Semitism may suggest. In fact, we were having a ball. London grew on me although I had hated it at first. I was overcome by its sheer size. I felt like an ant and developed a phobia which almost paralysed me. But little by little I overcame my problem, so much so that New York proved a walk-over when we had to move there three years later. I loved London after I had recovered from the first shock of living in a megalopolis. I came to adore its architecture, its history and tradition, its endless byways and magnificent shops, its beautiful parks, its sordidness and its snobbishness. But I could never forget, even for one second, the overt anti-Semitism that we were encountering in this land that I had been taught to honour as "the land of hope and glory, mother of the free"

Thus far we had only experienced "polite" anti-Semitism in our face to face encounters with the British. Before the end we were to be treated to the real thing. In all honesty we were asking for it and when it came we felt triumphant at having forced them out into the open. It became a challenge to us to do so and, in the end we succeeded and what is more we won the day.

It happened during the last months of our jobs in London. Over the last year a gigantic public controversy had been growing concerning the safety of the contraceptive pill, culminating in a Congressional Committee of Enquiry in Washington. Victor Wynn, an Australian

Jewish doctor, Professor of Human Metabolism at London University and a consultant to David's bureau in the ministry was the most outspoken authoritative voice in England calling for removal of the contraceptive Pill from the open market. The other side was spearheaded publicly by doctors Caroline and Malcom Potts, a husband and wife team. Sometime before the issue erupted into the media, Caroline Potts had consulted Victor Wynn as a private patient, because of the weight she herself was gaining due to the Pill. As the controversy over the safety of the Pill heated up personal relations became more and more strained. Professor Wynn documented dozens of bodily systems affected by the Pill and was invited to testify before the Committee of Inquiry in Washington. Caroline Potts responded to the media coverage she was receiving by giving her four-year-old daughter the contraceptive Pill, presumably in the tradition of Edward Jenner* and the cow pox virus.

* Edward Jenner injected an 8-year-old child with his newly discovered smallpox vaccine to demonstrate its effectiveness which bythen was encompassing the Women's Movement, the Catholic Church and big business interests

Caroline Potts responded to the media coverage she was receiving by giving her four-year-old daughter the contraceptive Pill, presumably in the tradition of Edward Jenner* and the cow pox virus.

She was soon accorded equal billing with Victor Wynn on television and in the press and the two medical adversaries became the public fronts of the escalating battle.

One evening at a cocktail party celebrating the conclusion of an International Planned Parenthood Foundation (IPPF) conference in Cambridge, the Potts's approached David with a request that he dismiss Victor Wynn from his position as consultant to the Population Bureau, claiming that Dr Wynn had attempted to rape Caroline during a private consultation with him some months previously. David was stunned. He questioned her about the consultation and what emerged was the description of a perfectly normal, competent and thorough medical examination. As it turned out from later investigation of the affair, the statutory witness required at such invasive examinations in the U.K. had also been present. Dr Wynn had apparently pummelled her adipose tissues on the breasts and buttocks as well as other less provocative areas of her body and this she had seen as an attempted rape. David told the Potts's that he considered what they had described to be a perfectly proper medical examination. Suddenly there were shrieks resounding over the party chatter and clinking of glasses:

"You Jew, you're nothing but a filthy Jew with your…" She was desperately searching for the diamond tie- pin or gold cufflinks and finding none blurted out instead " … your cigarettes and your first-class air travel!"

A hushed horror settled on the gathering and Malcom Potts led his wife away in tears. David and I were bewildered by this incident but not unduly upset. I remember waking the following morning expecting to find myself depressed by the affair, as one might have expected bruises to show up only hours after an accident. But I felt nothing. British anti-Semitism had by now become a puppet-show to us and we were now amusing ourselves, tweaking the strings.

On our return to London David informed Professor Wynn of this incident and advised him to take immediate legal action. Several days later two Indian doctors from the Family Planning Association (FPA) wrote to Victor Wynn informing him of the allegation of his attempted rape, being circulated by Malcom and Caroline Potts. Prof. Wynn responded with a solicitor's letter to the Potts's demanding a public retraction. Meanwhile I attended the continuation of the IPPF conference in London without David who had flown off to India the following week. A colleague of the Potts's refused to answer a question I addressed to him from the floor saying:

"I know what you're doing to the Potts's and I want nothing to do with you."

When David returned to hear this story, we too hastened to the solicitors to demand a retraction.

After much to-ing and fro-ing behind the scenes and with public libel actions about to be issued, private letters of retraction of all the allegations were received by the Indian doctors who had lodged complaints with the IPPF and Dr. Wynn. Mine, from the colleague who had snubbed me in public was accompanied by a profound and I think sincere letter, of apology.

We felt great satisfaction at this finale to our encounter with the anti-Semitism of the British establishment. As the British Bard might have concluded: "we exited content".

Note

The contents of this chapter prompted me to research the history of the Jews in England. I discovered that the British had never really felt very friendly towards us Jews. Having come to England first with William the Conqueror in 1066 it was all of fifty years before the pogroms started and from then until the European Enlightenment there seems to have been one continuous unmitigated merry-go-round of taxing most of the Jews into poverty and then shuffling them off into someone else's back yard; then bringing them back again to fill the landowners' coffers with more outrageously loaded taxing.

I learnt too that that most famous of all Christian projections, the blood libel, was invented in England in 1144.

From the time that David and I left England in 1972, it was to take almost 50 years before British Jewry finally found the courage to challenge anti-Semitism in their country. In November 2019, the Chief Rabbi of the United Kingdom published an article entitled "Utterly Betrayed", calling out the anti-Semitism in the British Labour Party, with polls predicting that 47% of British Jews would leave the country if Labour were elected in the forthcoming elections····.a heavy price to pay for not taking a stand against anti-Semitism all those years ago.

CHAPTER 13

AMERICA IS DIFFERENT

By comparison with the rest of Europe, British anti-Semitism was mild. After all, in my father's youth over a hundred Jewish communities were massacred in Czarist Russia; six million Jews died in Nazi Germany in the Second World War. So I imagine that Jews who had found a haven in England from such places would not understand why Jews like myself, coming from yet milder arenas, should find England so inhospitable. Years later, when living in Israel, I met Jews from Holland, (traditionally considered to be a friend of Israel), who told me in hushed whispers that the Dutch were no different, and Jews from Denmark, (whose population cooperated in saving the Danish Jews by evacuation to neutral Sweden), who gave the same account of the Danes.

The roots of anti-Semitism are contained in the Christian religion and therefore I have always assumed that anti-Semitism must be ubiquitous in all cultures founded on the Christian tradition, no matter what the prevailing political system may happen to be: Feudalism in Europe in the Middle Ages, egalitarianism in 18th century France, nationalism in 19th century Europe, or in the 20th century Communism Russia ,National Socialism in Germany, and Democracy in the Western World.

But America, American Jews claim, is different; the first exception to the rule of universal anti-Semitism in the entire history of Christianity.

We had met Sam Wishik and his wife Bel at a conference in London in 1970. They were a delightfully warm and, as far as we knew, Jewish couple in their late sixties. He was a well-known personality in population circles. She was a professor of sociology at New York

University. Sam had offered David and me positions in his International Institute for the Study of Human Reproduction in New York. We were overjoyed with the prospect of a chance to spend some time in the States and arranged to start after our contracts in England expired.

We arrived in New York in the fall of 1971 after a month's holiday in Australia. David had left Australia a month ahead of us to blaze the trail and arrived to meet me and the children (Aviva our 2-year-old daughter and Debbie my 14-year-old daughter by my first marriage) at Kennedy airport in an enormous spanking new yellow Buick convertible. With our three-year stints in each country we had by now learnt to adapt to the prevailing culture quickly. We soon shed our previously acquired English discretion and "good taste". We were stepping into the ultimate consumer society of flamboyance and kitsch. The new gleaming petrol guzzling eight-cylinder Buick cost less than we had received for our derelict second-hand Volvo in London.

Next came the perennial education in real estate. We decided to look in New Jersey not too far from the George Washington Bridge as the Institute was located nearby on the Manhattan side. The counties facing New York City on the opposite side of the Hudson River looked like the closest thing to Paradise that we had ever seen; magnificent homes set in carefully preserved natural surroundings, many with private swimming pools and tennis courts. There were plenty available for rental, but anything clean and decent was exorbitantly expensive. The real estate market was in the doldrums, and money was the cheapest commodity of all in this depressed economy. We could buy a house on ten percent deposit and borrow the rest at very low interest, repaying over twenty years. This was far cheaper than renting and most houses for sale were much nicer than those available for rent.

We chose a doll's house which could have come straight out of Home Beautiful, three miles from the George Washington Bridge in tiny Leonia, a township one square mile in area. The house, small by American standards, had three levels. Apart from carpets and drapes and light fittings, we had to furnish it completely. The Americans had a national past-time, almost as popular as baseball, of redecorating their homes. Any day of the week the local New Jersey papers carried pages and pages of used household furniture for sale. We furnished the entire house this way. But labour was fiendishly expensive. Transporting the furniture which we were buying cost more than the goods and the goods were not junk - far from it. We bought fine solid wood reproduction suites of maple and mahogany. We turned our convertible Buick into a furniture van by lowering the hood and balancing even a dining table or a wardrobe across the back seat. The bedrooms were so big that each member of the family ended up with a queen-size bed and our bedroom had two! Television sets cost less than half of what we had had to pay in London - the children each got a black-and-white one out of their pocket money. Goods, goods, goods poured into the house. We went mad like children let loose at a country fair.

We moved into the house within a week of signing the contract and with the same super speed, slid into the American way of life. At the end of the second week we had to go out and buy two jumbo-sized garbage bins to accommodate the waste we were generating every three days between the twice weekly garbage collections. Everything came super-sized and disposable; milk cartons in gallons, not litres; frozen vegetables in cellulose containers; butter in plastic tubs; cheese and pantyhose, cookies and men's shirts, cooking oil and coca cola; everything was packaged in throw-away containers. Then there were newspapers; mountains of newspapers. The Sunday Times ran to over one hundred and fifty pages! Piles of unsolicited advertisements were deposited in our letter box and when that overflowed, on the doormat in front of the house. For the first time in my life I had a garden to tend. By the end of our stay I had more gadgets and gimmicks for cutting lawns, trimming edges, shearing hedges, sucking up leaves, fertilising shrubs and watering plants than a normal hardware store in any other country would need to go into business. Every time you entered a supermarket you were confronted with a plethora of goods, cheap as chips, to make a healthier, more beautiful, more youthful, more athletic, more glamorous you. And when you had achieved this transformation you could start re-clothing your new image for next to nothing, in artificial silks and satins, suedes and leathers to match the stars of television or Hollywood. And when you looked like them you could set about smelling as you might imagine they ought to smell with a choice of hundreds of mouthwashes, underarm deodorants, vaginal sprays and foot powders.

We accumulated possessions till we could hardly fit into our three-storeyed house. Within a year it looked like most of the houses we had inspected a year earlier for purchase. Cupboards bulged, the attic was clogged up, we bought a prefabricated do-it-yourself out-house assembly kit to accommodate the overflow. Eventually, supersaturated with gadgets to compensate for the lack of services in this country, I was ready to start work at the Institute.

From the very first moment that I started to interact with American society, I felt that America *was* different. Cultural divisions cut across old familiar boundaries. More than 50% of our colleagues in the office were Jewish, but there were no "we" and "they" divisions here. There were pro- and anti-Sam Wishik factions. There was a militantly active Women's Lib cell. There were Republicans and Democrats sorely divided by the Vietnam War and the emerging Nixon scandal. But there was no time in our whole three years in New York when our ranks divided along the old familiar Jewish line. I did not even know till well into my second year in the Institute who all the Jews were. We made friends without regard to Jew or Gentile.

In New York Jews form one of the largest minority groups. I soon realised that many of the familiar distinguishing characteristics that I had always associated with Diaspora Jews did not apply here. In New York the Jews appear to have become a "normal" people. Various parts of the city and its environs were clearly divided ethnically. But where they came together, such as in our microcosmic Institute, the social demarcations shook down into different categories: scientists, bureaucrats, counter-culture freaks, militant protagonists of this or that cause, but not Jew and Gentile. Anti-Semitism and political Jewish issues seem to disappear. The news media were solidly pro-Israel; I even got to feel sorry for the Muslims who must have been feeling the frustrations we felt in England. I never once heard or saw an anti-Semitic remark or graffiti or article, nothing! There had been racial tension between Blacks and Jews in the sixties but I saw no evidence of this by the time we arrived in the early seventies.

In New York the Jews themselves seemed different, no doubt because of these vastly different influences acting upon them. Here we had the unique chance to observe a Jewish community large enough to perpetuate itself and retain its identity, living in a benign milieu without the restraining force of anti-Semitism holding it together. A major difference from the other communities that I had experienced was that I was almost completely incapable of distinguishing Jews from Gentiles unless they were physically identifiable as Jews and that was rarely the case. Assumptions I made, consciously or unconsciously, were usually wrong. When I tried to analyse why I had erred I discovered that I had usually assumed that the people I clicked with were Jewish. This was understandable from past experience, but what was not so readily explicable was that more often than not, the people I empathised with in New York were usually ***not*** Jewish!

I found an explanation after the event. On closer scrutiny the Gentiles, or at least many of those that I met, had taken on the characteristics of Jews, while the Jews had taken on characteristics of Gentiles. Yiddish words like *schlep* (to drag) and *schlemozzle* (stupid), *maven* (a guru) were in the New York vernacular and chicken soup and matza balls were on menus in many Gentile restaurants.

Within the Institute we were caught up in the passions of American society. The big issue of the day was Women's Lib and in our office were two national leaders of the movement: Harriet was Jewish, and Emily was not. Had I been I asked to identify which was which I would have failed. Harriet was blond and Emily was dark. Beyond this there were no other clues. Both were highly neurotic divorcees. They were as phobic on the issue of male domination as any Jew I had ever encountered on the issue of anti-Semitism. My closest friend in the Institute was Benny Pasquerella, a Catholic Hispanic American with the most superb Jewish sense of humour. Don Helbig a Dutch American doctor and his wife , both looked Jewish but turned out not to be. They were into nudity and a return to nature. We were invited to glorious weekends at their Hamish retreat in the Pennsylvanian countryside where after five minutes of acute embarrassment, thousands of years of inhibition really did dissolve into nothingness. They did not invite everyone to the retreat, some fitted, some did not, but again this dividing line did nothing to demarcate Jews from Gentiles. Our scapegoat in the Institute was a Jew (married to a Gentile) ; the suspected CIA plant from Washington, who reported on our internal policy meetings to the powers that held the purse-strings in Washington.

Martin, the handsome young demographer was married to Susan, a beautiful social worker. They were childhood sweethearts, both Jewish, a picture of smiling health and youthful energy. We got to know them very well. Unable to have children themselves, they had adopted two non-Jewish children, whom they were dutifully raising as secular but staunch Jews. Martin was rising quickly in his profession, but the further he climbed, the greater grew Susan's hostility towards him. All the frustrations of raising babies in the heart of Manhattan, all her regrets at marrying her first boyfriend, were channelled via the Women's Liberation movement into resentment of her husband's professional success. The situation viewed from outside the marriage was bizarre. He did as much, if not more than she, in caring for the children and running the home. She decided she wanted another profession. Martin supported her and ran the home and cared for the children through her architecture course. She needed an analyst (as did most people that we met in New York). He almost bankrupted himself paying for it. In the end, qualified and analysed, she left him. The children were launched upon the newest American fad of half the week with him, half the week with her. Before long, each parent had a new flatmate, each with his and her own half share of another set of kids. It was the new American version of the extended family. America **was** different!!

Sam Wishik, whom I had regarded as a father-figure - he even looked like my father - was born Jewish, but now belonged to the Unitarian Church. I could not reconcile him to this faith, try as I did. He was to me as my father had said of himself, an "alter Yid", an old Jew. His wife Bel was fiercely Zionistic. There seemed to be a concerted effort to smash all preconceived boundaries. To us it was a madhouse, but tremendously exciting and stimulating.

I felt that Americans took themselves grotesquely seriously, that is at least the middle-class professionals that we were meeting. They seemed to need to create the problems of life necessary to give it meaning. The Women's Liberation Movement tackled many real issues, still pertinent to the emancipation of women. But

"Women's Lib" was much more. It was a religion complete with martyrs and saints and a huge persecution complex. The persecutors were the male chauvinists and the victims, all women. Women were designated as a minority with total disregard for the actual meaning of the words "chauvinist" or "minority". The high priestesses of the religion roused their persecuted "minority" to battle and warned that blood would flow before the battle was over. I was invited to join our regiment in the Institute with a rhetorical question from its field commander: "Does any man have any idea of the pain and trauma of a girl's first period?" She said it with the gravity appropriate to a discussion on victims of a genocide. I could not take them seriously, but I soon learnt how serious they were. I hardly met an American, man or woman over the next three years who did not regard the Women's Cause as sacrosanct. Men were seen to persecute women in America, as Cossacks had persecuted Jews in Russia, but no Jewish/Gentile divide here.

It was not only women who were struggling for their rights: children, the disabled, the left-handed, fat people and finally the cause of animal Lib each took the stage during our stay. The Blacks had already had their big push in the fifties and sixties. Everyone had had a turn except the Jews. They had simply overcome the quite intense discrimination practiced against them early in the century by their wits. Now they found the process working against them by default. An anti-discrimination law was passed to enforce equal representation of all minority groups in many highly competitive jobs such as university staffs, members of Parliament and civil servants etc; but paradoxically, Jews were threatened by it. Applicants had to be considered first by race, sex and colour and only then by merit. But Jews were enormously overrepresented in these spheres. The result was that Jews were, by default, being selectively denied access to university appointments. Numerus Clausus, U.S. style!!

The Jews of America were now moving toward the Jewish ideal of the European Enlightenment: to become American citizens of the Mosaic faith.

This process was well advanced in the smaller communities. We saw it clearly when we visited friends who had immigrated to the States from Australia twenty years previously. Herbert and Vera lived in Iowa where they belonged to the Reform synagogue. Their behaviour and life- style, except for the occasional visit to Israel, are indistinguishable from that of Gentile Americans. They took us to see their new synagogue as a highlight of our visit to the bread-basket of America. There, crowning the fields of golden corn were two houses of worship on the top of a gentle hill; the one Jewish, the other Episcopalian. The two congregations had purchased the land jointly, built their houses to match architecturally and shared their furniture in the early days moving chairs across on Saturdays to the synagogue and on Sundays to the church. They invited each other to participate in social activities and conducted all praying in English.

American Jews are the most intensely patriotic of all the Jews I have ever met. They really do feel that America is their land. I shall never forget the Jewish woman on the plane coming in to land at Kennedy Airport on a direct flight from Tel Aviv, who exclaimed in joy "Isn't it nice to get back to your own country again!" Whether they can remain Jews in the face of such unimpeded freedom and whether this unimpeded freedom can last forever, only the future will tell. If they do and if it does, then America will indeed be different from anything yet encountered in the long history of the Jews.

Our careers in population control lasted for nine years until political manoeuvring and then racism, began to foul our "holy mission". Population control became first a capitalist conspiracy and then a white man's plot. One by one the most prestigious organizations involved in population work succumbed to the New Left in the Third World and ultimately Arab oil politics. The United Nations started curtailing population activities and finally crowned its efforts for the International Year of the Child, , with a stark racist poster depicting fat, overfed white babies eating apples from the tree of life, with hollow-eyed, undernourished black babies looking on. The Department where we were currently employed by Columbia University in New York, changed its name from the "International Institute for Human Reproduction" to "Centre for Family Help". David walked out of the 1975 Stockholm World Medical Organisation Conference on Population, which was turned into an undiluted, insulting attack on the white delegates by the non-whites.

A combination of factors finally cast the die. We felt frustrated by the growing political opposition in Third World countries to First World population control programs. We also felt embarrassed to continue to hold our jobs while American colleagues in our own Institute were being laid off because of the threatening recession in the United States. Finally, we were also angered by the increasingly obvious sell-out of Israel by the Third World countries in which we were working, in the arse-licking race for Arab oil. We had become disillusioned with our messianic dreams like innumerable idealists before us. We decided to quit the population field.

From a personal point of view, we were not unhappy with the decision. We yearned for a more settled life. Our 5-year-old daughter Aviva, born in London, had already been to a dozen different kindergartens. David wanted to write a book on the world population problem. Apart from that we had no plans. We wanted to drift for a while and see where we landed

CHAPTER 16

THE SECOND COMING

We flew home to Melbourne for a holiday, rented an old house with the most beautiful swimming pool and soon fell into a life of ease and luxury that we had never before had the time to enjoy. At the end of the summer I suggested a visit to Israel before we got involved with jobs again. It was June and therefore hot in Israel, so we travelled light, not even filling the allowed twenty kilos per person. We both knew that we were going to take a long-range look at Israel. But neither of us really had the foggiest notion what exactly we were looking for.

We returned to Israel in June 1977, one month short of a quarter of a century after I had left with Geoff in such disarray. I seemed to need a second chance at everything. My mother said, when I was about to change husbands, that I could not even buy a pair of shoes without changing them for another. In the intervening twenty-five years I had tallied up two professions, two husbands, two families and now perhaps two *aliyot* (immigrations to Israel)

We stayed as tourists for two years. For the first three months we camped in student digs in Ramat Eshkol, a suburb of Jerusalem. Accommodation was an enormous problem in Jerusalem by the end of 1977. For the first time since the establishment of the State in 1948, the Labour party had just lost an election and with the right-wing Likud party in power, Israel was heading for an economic boom. The government introduced sweeping economic reform to encourage overseas investment and in response money flowed into the country. The whole world seemed to be coming to Israel: wealthy Jews from

France were madly buying apartments as insurance policies against the rising Muslim immigration to France; it was the in-place for Scandinavians and German students for a working holiday; there was a steady rise in immigration from troubled Iran and South Africa; every other American professor was spending his sabbatical here.

The native Israelis were stunned.

"Why on earth should you want to come here from Australia? I want to go there" a young native-born Israeli taxi driver told me. I started to expound on the spiritual wealth of Israel and the bankruptcy of the decaying West; on the need to belong and the lack of direction of Jewish youth in the Diaspora. His look conveyed his assessment of me as an over-indulged Anglo-Saxon gone soft. He had no idea what I was talking about, never having experienced a country in which he did not belong, nor a life of material ease.

"Let's swap for a while" was his parting remark as he handed me the change.

I didn't know it then but that is just what we were doing. There was a silent low-profile increasing *yerida* (emigration out of Israel), the extent of which was only to become public knowledge around the beginning of 1979.

Who were the "crazies" flocking to Israel in the seventies? There were several rational reasons for immigrating to Israel. One was quite simply that there wasn't anywhere else to go. This, to many is Israel's primary *raison d'etre*. This was the case with many Holocaust survivors immediately after World War II and subsequent refugees from the Arab countries. Then there were the Zionists who came because they believed that the Jews should have a land of their own and live in it. A third category consisted of religious Jews who felt that they could live a better religious life in a country whose official religion is Jewish.

There was also a steadily growing immigration of people in search of themselves. They were people in crisis; people of all ages, seeking roots and direction in the Jewish historical homeland ; young *baalei teshuva* (literally "returnees to the way") consisting largely of spiritually disenchanted American youngsters trying a return to the orthodoxy of their grandparents; Jewish divorcees and widows, hoping to find spouses; a motley collection of Christian converts to Judaism; Christian sects with their own versions of messianism, which somehow involved the return of the Jews to Zion; black Hebrews who believed themselves to be the only true Jews; Christians attempting to exculpate post-Holocaust feelings of guilt or to reconcile the rifts between Judaism and Christianity; missionaries overtly or covertly still pursuing the age-old Christian crusade to win Jewish souls for Jesus; Jewish criminals attempting to exercise their right of return in order to escape the law; black *Falashas* staking their claim as Jews and finally winning.

By September we still had not found whatever it was that we were looking for, so we decided to extend our stay and we started digging in for the approaching winter. To our dismay practically all furnished rental accommodation in Jerusalem had been snapped up due to the sudden increase in immigration When we arrived in June there had been plenty available and we had taken the first clean and reasonably priced apartment we saw without much regard to comfort or location. It had two bedrooms, one of which immediately became superfluous as Aviva, scared out of her wits by the bomb drills for children at school insisted on sleeping in our bed anyway. The week we moved in there had been a mobile travelling exhibition in the neighbourhood of booby traps planted by PLO terrorists in the streets of Jerusalem. These included sweets, dolls, toy cars, money, loaves of bread discarded in rubbish cans and so on. Compounding her terror, on our third day in the apartment there was a minor earth tremor. Our flat was located in Ramat Eshkol which is itself a high plateau and we were on the fourth floor (without a lift). Because of the elevated height the effect of the minor tremor was magnified to the extent that furniture shook and crockery broke. That sealed all our efforts to reassure the child and it took six months to get her back into her own bed again.

We moved four times in the next year. It was like the story of Goldilocks - one apartment was too cold (but big enough), another too high (without a lift), the third was too small (but warm enough), until one day we found one just big enough, warm enough and with an elevator. Moving in and out of apartments in Israel involved more legal work than buying a house in America or Australia. The main problem seemed to be telephones. There was a five year wait to reconnect a telephone, so they remained connected in the original owner's names forever. We now receive accounts addressed to Mr. Shazar, a former deceased President of Israel! To cover themselves against unpaid bills by tenants, landlords demanded thousands of dollars' worth of securities. The pettiness was soul-destroying. We got embroiled in disputes over the value of a scratch on a dining-room table or a broken cup. In America we had bought and completely furnished our house in a month. In Israel it took us three years to complete the same task.

By the time our indefinite stay had extended into its fourth year we decided that we might as well assume immigrant status and settle in more comfortably. We rented an unfurnished apartment and faced the horrendous job of buying our own furnishings. As new immigrants we were allowed to buy or import furnishings duty-free. Most Western immigrants opt to bring their furnishings in a shipment from their country of origin but then run into a bureaucratic nightmare with shipping agents, insurance agents, customs clearance and road transport from the docks. We decided to buy locally instead. We spent hours, days, weeks, finally months running back and forth, returning goods which did not match order samples, or broke down under guarantee. Our lives became filled with nonsense.

Our social intercourse was reduced to comparing nightmares and relieving frustrations by venting our hatred against sadistic Israeli petty officials and unscrupulous businessmen. The clash of Western expectations and Oriental inefficiency produced sparks which ignited into smouldering resentments and even open hostilities. I saw reserved Englishmen behaving like wild animals in the infamous *"meches"* (customs) building in Keren Hayesod Street, in Jerusalem. Like many new immigrants from Western societies before us, we soon came to regard Israeli petty officials as storm-troopers. I myself was twice provoked into so losing my temper that I called them just that, which in turn unleashed the wrath of Hell on my head. I soon learnt that in Israel comparison with the Nazis was as taboo as reference to Colour had been in Singapore.

We came to accept visits to the *meches* (customs) department as an unavoidable daily routine of life. And after finally bidding farewell to the "meches" department, we had to accept quadrupling the proportion of our time normally devoted to bureaucracy. Only then could we start to face life with regained poise and equanimity and to acquire the Israeli mentality summed up in the Hebrew expression *"yehiye tov"* (all will be well).

There was no unemployment in Israel at that time, being a pioneering country constantly at war. But the types of jobs readily available to new immigrants were mainly unskilled or in pioneering outposts. In a country whose population was doubling every five years veteran Israelis rightly expected to retain their positions in the workplace. Consequently, the new arrivals had to take a dive and climb back up the ladder slowly. However, this posed a serious problem for both the new arrivals and the country. Israel consistently robbed herself of the enormous profitability of utilising the skills of new immigrants many of whom had reached the pinnacle of their careers before immigrating to Israel.

My friend Benny ran a chain of twenty retail outlets in Birmingham. He had immigrated to Israel because his two sons were now living there with all his grandchildren. He offered his services voluntarily and became involved in reorganising not-for-profit shops appended to institutions such as museums and hospitals. After a year he had doubled the takings of the Israel Museum's souvenir sales. I watched him tear his hair out one by one, struggling with the incompetence of those with authority over him who had never before sold a lollypop in their whole lives. He patiently battled on in the sure conviction that when he had proven his value, he would be given authority to carry on unfettered by the incompetence of those currently running the show. But this did not happen and unwilling to stand by helplessly while thousands of dollars were squandered by inefficiency he resigned in disgust, to face his twilight years in idleness and boredom.

Pierre from Paris owned an international dried fruit empire. Both his children had settled in Israel and he wanted nothing more than to follow them here. He spent a year trying to donate his worldwide connections to Israel in return for a government job in which he would have sufficient autonomy to salvage Israel's enormous dumped fruit crops of "seconds" and seasonal over-production. In his mid-forties he was too young to retire He left the country broken-hearted and disillusioned after months of unsuccessful negotiations with the Ministry of Agriculture.

By the time we left the population field, David was considered a leading authority on the subject. He presented the Israeli government with a proposal for a maternal and child health care centred contraceptive program which they welcomed. Contrary to popular belief Israel had an urgent need for such a program despite its pronatalist policy. The poor sections of society needed contraceptive services, the religious wanted to control their spacing of children and were allowed to by Rabbinic decree. There was also a possibility of political complications because Israel could be accused of trying to curb the increase in Arab populations living under Israeli jurisdiction. The Arabs were suffering one of the highest birth rates in the world. While this high birth rate among the Muslim population may have been seen as threatening Israel with demographic catastrophe, the absence of a family planning program would have denied Israeli Muslims as well as those under Israeli administration in the disputed territories, the humane right to limit their family size which Muslims in Egypt, Tunisia, Morocco and Algeria enjoyed. There were in fact at that time, World Health Organisation contraceptive programmes operating in most Muslim countries.

David started work on this program, in March 1978 with full cooperation of the director of health services and the blessing of the Israeli government. He quit after six weeks. To his amazement he found that he had to work, not in cooperation with, but under the authority of, the director of the child and maternal health centres, a middle aged Russian woman, who had held this position for fifteen years and who had not the foggiest notion of what a contraceptive program entailed. He resigned like so many others we met, not out of hurt pride, but because of the inability to function efficiently, if at all. The list of casualties was long and the loss to Israel inestimable. This recipe for inefficiency was a legacy of the early socialist ideology of the country which still persisted thanks to the policy of the *Histadrut*, the national trade-union, that decreed that once in, you can never be forced out and no one ever leaves except of his or her own volition or with an extremely high severance payout.

Israel, especially Jerusalem, was sorely divided by religious issues. Here to the orthodox, the secular Jew was a bit of a *goy* (a gentile). Social relations were determined primarily along the dimension of religiosity. The first question the neighbour's kids asked my little girl when we moved into our new apartment was: "are you *'datiah"* (religious)? The public-school system was similarly divided into two streams for the Jewish population - religious and secular. (There was a third stream for Arabs.) Religious Jews lived in segregated areas, forced there by the very rules once designed to segregate them from the gentiles. Even in our non-religious areas certain buildings were designated *"dati"* and prohibited the use of cars and elevators on the Sabbath. Even within the building that I lived in a social divide existed between those who did and those who did not observe the Sabbath, immediately identifiable by their use of the stairs or elevator on Saturdays.

The dietary laws effectively kept the observant out of secular homes. Ironically, in Jerusalem I was isolated even from Australian Jews with whom I could easily have socialised in the diluted religiosity of the Diaspora. In Sydney and Melbourne observant Jews could tolerate meatless meals in non-kosher households, or non-observant visitors arriving by car or tram to their homes on the Sabbath. But in Jerusalem, where we were only a local phone call from God, the rules were more stringently observed. Those who had been united in the Diaspora by the Jewish prayer "Next year in Jerusalem" were here often divided in its realisation.

One did not gain immediate acceptance in Israel by virtue of the law of return. One gained only immediate citizenship. There are resentments and jealousies, factions and divisions in Israeli society as in any other. The only real difference, and it was an enormous one, was that one could be certain that anti-Semitism played no part in them. But every other social bias and bigotry did - economic, religious and cultural.

The Western new immigrants to Israel were resented and rejected by the "old-timers" of both Western and Oriental origins. They resented their comparative wealth and immigrant privileges such as rights to tax-free goods which they themselves had never enjoyed. They were impatient with the new immigrants' pre-occupation with their problems of integration. They were intolerant of the newcomers criticisms and resisted their intrusions. The sincere and effective help that Diaspora

Jewish communities traditionally provided for new Jewish immigrants to their own homelands in the Diaspora, was here replaced by a cold and inefficient bureaucracy. Immigrants from advanced Western countries got financial assistance that they often did not need, but they were jealously obstructed in obtaining work commensurate with their skills and experience which was vital for them.

After three years in Israel we were further from integration into this society than we had been when we arrived. Surrounded by a majority of Oriental and religious Jews in Jerusalem, we often felt more alienated in Israel than in the Diaspora. Furthermore, we were also now personally experiencing Israel's international isolation, rather than just hearing or reading about it in the media. Each morning we woke to more condemnations by the United Nations and more trade boycotts. One day the half dozen odd remaining foreign embassies in Jerusalem packed their bags and moved to Tel Aviv. I noticed a strange thing; veteran Israelis were not nearly as upset by all this rejection as we newcomers.

But while Israelis often appeared indifferent to outside political pressures, they were often critical of Diaspora Jewry. Just as I sensed that to the ultra-religious Jews the secular Jew was a bit of a *goy*, so to the Israelis any Jew who did not come to live in Israel was now less of a Jew.

There is a Hebrew Zionist song which starts:

"Let us turn our faces to Israel"

which Israelis vulgarized in the sixties by adding

"and our arses to the Diaspora".

Tragically, this antagonism had resulted in the Israelis adopting the Gentile anti-Semitic image of the Diaspora Jew. I took Aviva to see the film version of Oliver Twist in Jerusalem. I had studied the book in high-school but I could not remember ever having raised an objection to Fagin in class. I never asked why he looked and behaved like no Jew I had ever met or why I should have felt myself in any way responsible and guilty, which I did, for this loathsome devil of a Jew. But not so my Aviva. She attacked Fagin the moment we left the cinema and so I explained, as best I could to an eight-year-old, how Christian anti-Semitism had created this stereotype of the Jew as the Devil. But talking to an Israeli friend about this incident the next day evinced a startling reaction: her children, would have no problem with Fagin she claimed. They knew that due to oppression and persecution that is how Jews behave in the Diaspora and now Jews need no longer be like that because we had Israel!

I was flabbergasted. To me Diaspora Jewry represented the mainstream of the Jewish people, its culture the only Judaism I had ever known. To me Israel's purpose was to preserve the Diaspora, not to annihilate it. The Holocaust had succeeded with such devastating success because the Jewish people had had no organised voice to represent it, no army to defend it, no land to receive it and this must never again be allowed to happen. But I had never imagined for one moment that Israelis might think that Diaspora Jewry was not worth saving. I remembered reading somewhere that Ben Gurion, on the eve of WWII when confronted with the task of aiding European Jewry, once said (to his shame in my opinion) that he would rather save one Jewish child in Israel than ten in Europe.

Nor was this attitude rare amongst Israelis. The general response in Israel to the unleashing of anti-Semitic terror around the world during the Israel-Lebanese campaign, was "let them come here if they don't like it". The suggestion that Israel should take into account the consequences that her actions to protect herself may have on Diaspora Jewry was, quite rightly, unacceptable to Israelis but in my opinion for the wrong reason. It was right because history had shown that anti-Semitism functioned independently of Jewish behaviour. There had been a slow but steady resurgence of anti-Semitism in the Diaspora since World War II which was at that time again readying to erupt into the open, due to current political and economic conditions in the Western world. Israel's campaign into the Lebanon had provided the excuse, not the cause, for its timing. It was right that Israel should have placed her national security first in such circumstances, indeed in any circumstances. But not because Israelis were better, more righteous, more deserving or more precious than Diaspora Jews, but because Israel's security was also Diaspora Jewry's only insurance policy, because only a strong Israel could save the Diaspora from future holocausts.

I estimate that only one in ten Israelis that I had spoken with, saw Israel's relationship to the Diaspora in this way. The other nine simply denied the legitimacy of any claim on Israel of any Jew who did not immigrate to Israel.

On the other hand, the political and financial support of world Jewry for Israel was quite rightly expected by Israelis. Israel's policy of unrestricted immigration to Diaspora Jews placed a moral, financial and political responsibility on them. Israelis risked their lives and gave years of service in the defence of this country to provide Diaspora Jews, even anti-Zionists, with an escape route from physical annihilation and a political voice in the international arena. These functions had already been put to the test in the struggle to save Ethiopian and Soviet Jewry.

All the Jews in the world are not going to immigrate to Israel, nor, in my opinion, would this be desirable. Diaspora Jewry embodies a unique and superb culture which Israel will continue to draw upon and contribute to in a symbiotic relationship which neither can avoid. The Jews are one people wherever they live and whenever we have forgotten this the rest of the world has soon reminded us of it.

As a child I had always felt cheated by Bible stories. I was sceptical of all those miracles that only ever happened in the way distant past. But in Jerusalem I learnt that it didn't really matter that I had missed out on witnessing all those ancient miracles which happened too long ago for anybody to verify. I found to my amazement that the Jewish religion did not require me to believe the veracity of a single miracle; in fact, I did not even have to accept the existence of God. I did not have to ***believe*** in anything

I discovered that the Jews had made a contract with their God, whereby they undertook to obey His commandments and He in return undertook to take care of them, His Chosen People. The only essential difference between the Jewish believer and the Jewish atheist is that the believer assumes God created man and this contract between Himself and His Chosen People, while the atheist believes that **man** created both God and his contract with the Jewish people. This is what led a delegate to the 1981 Jewish American Congress in Jerusalem to introduce himself as "a secular religious Jew".

I enrolled for classes in Bible study at the Hebrew University. I was overawed by what I learnt there. The drama, the history and the philosophy which I began to discover in our Book held me spellbound. I was fascinated by my own predilection to see the world the way our Bible views it. My childhood home was totally devoid of Jewish tradition and Jewish religion. Yet when I finally confronted the Jewish Bible as a Jewish agnostic, I found myself able to empathise with its view of the universe and of humanity, with its logic and its morality.

I recognized my own thoughts in the writings of some old Jew, three thousand years dead! I came to suspect that the Bible may be the link that still united the Jews in a secular world, even those who like myself were ignorant of it. Maybe this was the "something, at the very heart of (him)" that Freud could not identify.

Since Jesus was little known in his time, little was recorded contemporaneously of his birth, life and death? However, some people have decided with great conviction on the exact spot of his birth and marked it by a hole in the ground about six inches in diameter. It is located in an underground vault above which Christians have built the Church of the Nativity in Bethlehem. When I first visited it some years ago I had been deeply moved. We had filed in a single silent line down into the vault with a motley crowd of cripples, hippies draped in sheets to cover exposed limbs and old people preparing to face their Creator. We had moved slowly down a winding staircase cut out of the rock wall into the stuffy, airless pitch-black vault where a single red light glowed from inside the hole. It looked like the blood spot of a birth and the hole looked like the opening of a womb. The silence was the silence of a momentous event: **something had happened here which shook the world**.

I visited the vault again a year later. This time it was fully lit and packed like a sardine can with successive parties of noisy, babbling tourists: first a group of Africans, then Italians, then Spaniards. People were pushing and shoving for a glimpse of the "hole". I surfaced for air and waited till the crowds had gone. When I returned there was only a small party of Frenchmen left; three young anaemic slender men and eight elderly women. They were prostrating themselves in turn before the hole and burying their faces into it in order, I imagine, to inhale the stale air; a kiss on the circumference then up to make way for the next person. Two of them had brought bread wrapped in cloth which was passed over the opening, presumably to be ingested by some friend or relative on their return home.

I drove back to Jerusalem with the sun setting behind this unbelievable city of gold. Mosques were frantically calling the faithful to prayer. At the Western Wall black-clad Hassidic Jews were shrilly celebrating the exit of the Sabbath bride.

I detoured to the Old City to savour these contrasts to the full. On the top of the Temple Mount bare-footed Arabs were pressing head to ground in the worship of Allah. Below head-covered Jews were swaying back and forth at a stone wall. I huddled on the steps descending from the Jewish Quarter to the huge stone plaza in front of the Western Wall. In the summer months it had been packed with tourists on Friday and Saturday nights, but now it was deserted. The Wall rises like a colossus, embodying 2000 years of Jewish yearning for this city. Like ants, the tiny black figures of religious Jews were pressed hard against its base, some in actual physical embrace with the stones.

In my mind's eye I could see parading across the gigantic plaza in front of the Wall, all the generations that spanned the centuries between these tiny specks and their forefathers who stood in this same place worshipping this same God before He too dispersed with them on their journey to the ends of the earth.

The thought struck me, that in that whole two thousand years, there had probably not passed a single second in which some Jew somewhere in this world was not rising with the dawn to turn towards this Wall to pray.

CHAPTER 17

WHOSE MESSIAH? WHOSE JERUSALEM?

According to the Jewish religion, conversion to Judaism confers upon the convert full, even ancestral, acceptance within the Jewish fold. The biblical Sara is as much the matriarch of a convert as of any Jew born of a Jewish mother. Converts are also protected from discrimination by the Talmudic injunction that other Jews are forbidden from making reference to their status as a convert.

In Australia I had known one or two women who had converted to Judaism in order to marry Jewish men, but I had never met a person who had converted for any other reason. In Jerusalem I soon encountered half a dozen such converts and through them many more. They intrigued me, because Talmudic injunctions notwithstanding, I knew that they had not been made into "real Jews" by the act of conversion and within their margins of difference I felt there may be some clues to my own identity.

Ruth was an Irish American from the mid-West. I had met her at Hebrew class, bravely breaking her teeth over Hebrew vocabulary. There was a mystery about her past which only deepened the more I got to know her. She never received mail from the States, and she knew no one in Israel, other than me. As the months went by, I pieced together the following picture: she had been married to a man whom she only ever referred to as "the beast" .She had had two children by him, a boy and a girl, now in their late teens, who it seemed preferred to remain with "the beast" rather than live with her after the marriage broke up. During her ensuing loneliness and misery, she happened to read "The Source" by James Michener and Moshe Dayan's biography and on the strength of her fascination with these two books she had decided to convert to Judaism. I could hardly imagine how such a flimsy basis had sustained her through the arduous years of study that an orthodox conversion to Judaism entails, let alone the trials of integration into Israeli society that she was now encountering. She had turned herself into something as far removed as possible from what she was born. She had changed her name from Patricia to Ruth and not only was she now Jewish but fanatically religious and militantly Zionist. She knew far more about the Jewish religion than I and observed its ritual meticulously. But her blind acceptance of her new-found religion, the black and white and right and wrong of her Judaism struck me as the antithesis of the ambiguous "maybe" of *my* Judaism. Or as Tevia put it in Fiddler on the Roof "on the other hand"?

One day an Indian doctor friend, Nulla Tan, from Singapore came to visit us in Jerusalem. I invited her to lunch with Ruth and the three of us set out for an afternoon's sightseeing. Nulla was a devout Christian and naturally wanted to see something of Christian Jerusalem. We wandered around the Christian Quarter of the

Old City where we came across the Church of the Holy Sepulchre. Inside there is a chamber that I had never seen before containing a white slab of marble, on which the body of Jesus is believed by many Christians to have been laid after it was taken down from the cross. Ruth stopped dead at the door and refused to enter. I went in with Nulla. To my astonishment tears welled up in the eyes of this normally pragmatic, professional woman as she laid a trembling hand caressingly on the cold white stone.

Bunny's conversion was a pure act of identification. She had come to Jerusalem with a group of thirty Christian families which belonged to a movement called Bnei Shalom. They lived together in a communal society which emulated the economic and social structure of an Israeli kibbutz. They rented an entire apartment block in Jerusalem, cooked and ate communally, pooled their earnings and so forth. When I met Bunny, they were fighting a losing battle with the authorities for the right to permanent residence in Israel. They were plagued of course by the perennial suspicions of missionary activities. A year after her arrival in Israel, Bunny left the group and filed for an American divorce from her husband who was also in the group. She launched out on her own in Jerusalem and within another year and a half had converted to Judaism and mastered the Hebrew language. The transformation in personality and appearance was unbelievable. She changed from a mousy, pale-faced, drooping mid-Western American hillbilly into a rosy bouncing "with-it" Israeli.

"Why did you do it", I asked her when we met for coffee in downtown Jerusalem at the annual reunion of our Ulpan* class.

"My mother always told me to follow the Jews for they are the Chosen People. All great things in God's design will happen where they are, so always stay close to the Jews. So, I decided to take her advice".

*Ulpan: government run Hebrew classes for new migrants

I doubted that this was exactly what Bunny's mother had in mind but in the prevailing circumstances the only way that Bunny could stay close to the Jews was to become one of them. Bunny made a most convincing Jewess. She applied for and was granted Israeli citizenship, married a Sephardi Jew and I should imagine by now has added a couple of bouncing circumcised sons to the house of Israel.

Daniel was a celebrity convert. He had been written up several times in the Israeli press. I had also heard him tell the story of his conversion at a public lecture entitled "Jews by Choice".

He became a Jew because, although a religious Protestant, he felt that he was praying in a different way from all the other congregants in his Church. He had had no contact with Jews as a child but through his parents and grandparents he had learnt what had happened to the Jews during the Second World War. In his early twenties he moved to Dusseldorf and there he first met Jews. He was searching for another way to God and through his contact with them he started on the long and arduous path to Judaism.

After a year on the kibbutz he joined the course for converts run by the then chief Ashkenazi Rabbi of Israel, Rabbi Goren. After three separate interrogations he had convinced the rabbi that he was a suitable candidate for conversion he then had to embark upon a difficult course of instruction, undergo circumcision and the ritual submersion before admission to the Jewish faith.

Not long afterward at one of his public lectures I heard Daniel delivering some words of wisdom to the Jewish people:

"We are being severely punished now" he explained, "because the vast majority of Jews have forgotten the laws of Moses."

He exhorted us all to return to the righteous path of strict observance of the laws of Moses and the true Messiah would appear.

As there are seldom less than a dozen crazies at any time in Jerusalem claiming to be the Messiah, I wondered if in the unlikely event that the Jews did all return to the righteous path, how we would know which was the real McCoy? But I decided not to complicate Daniel's sermon as the question was purely academic since there was little chance of many Israelis concerning themselves with the laws of Moses any time soon.

Our encounter with Aaron was short but very interesting. David had taken a typed manuscript to a printing press in downtown Jerusalem for copying and we had gone together to pick it up a few days later. When we arrived in the rather messy shed hidden away in an alley behind Hillel Street we were greeted by an excited young man in his late twenties:

"I'm sorry" he said, "but I could not print your manuscript, so you will need to take it elsewhere."

"Why not?" asked David, a little annoyed at the loss of a week.

"Because my rabbi said it was not permitted to question the Masoretic text."

"Which rabbi told you that?" David demanded. The poor fellow caved in and admitted that that was not exactly what the rabbi had said.

"So, what exactly did the rabbi tell you?" asked David.

"He told me I must decide for myself what the Bible teaches me is right and wrong."

Oh Catholic, Catholic Jew!

Oh Jewish, Jewish Rabbi!

For me outside Israel Christianity had always been not only a religion but also a culture against which I was forever measuring myself. But in Israel Christianity was only a religion and here Christians for me were simply people who believe that Jesus is the Messiah, God's only begotten son and that he has already visited us here on earth and that he would come again. They were not light versus dark, strong versus weak, good versus bad, generous versus miserly, day versus night as they were in my adolescence. They were not people against whom I had to measure my performance, to whom I must adjust my behaviour, from whom I must hide my sins. They were just people who were, for the first time in my life, lowered to my strength and raised to my intelligence. In Jerusalem I was attracted to their centres and their interests. I was moved by their religious ecstasy and puzzled by their fascination with us. For here we were both on equal playing grounds and it was an intriguing contrast and interplay

.Most Christians who lived in Jerusalem, at that time either hated us or loved us. There was a small group of in-between Christians who neither hated nor loved us but wanted to convert us.

The haters were in general the representatives of traditional Christianity in this Holy City. There was hostility between the Orthodox Greek and Russian clergies and the municipality of Jerusalem which was kept on a low profile. Nor was there much love lost between us and the other Christian sects, Roman Catholics, Scottish Presbyterians and so forth. But relations with these contacts were mainly formal between consulates, looking after political interests. Teddy Kollek, the Mayor of Jerusalem, treated them like all other foreign minorities with vested interests in this city with an aim to keep the peace and protect the rights of all.

The lovers were the Christian Fundamentalists. This new turn of events amongst some of their sixty million adherents throughout the world was one of the most exciting developments in the history of Judea-Christian relationships. It started formally in 1980 when the last foreign embassy relocated out of Jerusalem to Tel Aviv in protest against Israel's annexation of the Golan Heights. A group of Christian Fundamentalists moved into the magnificent, vacated premises of the former Chilean Embassy and proclaimed themselves the International Christian Embassy. They have since gone from strength to strength, politically, financially and spiritually.

On entering the splendid mansion that houses the Christian Embassy in Jerusalem one sensed an atmosphere of zealous mission and dedication, almost fanatical in its intensity. The staff of twenty, drawn from a dozen different countries, ran great physical risk from terrorist attacks, because of the political statement that the very existence of their embassy in Jerusalem implied. Nevertheless, the imposing front door was never locked. In response to its chiming bell, it was opened without guard or security check to anyone seeking admission. The main hall of the Embassy was decorated with magnificent huge hand-embroidered murals, proclaiming their unqualified devotion to their sacred cause - Zionism.

"Comfort ye, comfort ye My people!" commanded God through his prophet Isiah and now from the walls of the Christian Embassy.

The driving force behind this movement was the Reverend Van der Hoeven, one of the founders of the Christian Embassy. Formerly curator of the Garden Tomb where Jesus is believed to have been buried, he had lived in Israel for fifteen years. He left his native Holland in disgust with the decay of Christian values in the Western world, determined to do something about it. As a Christian he interpreted the Bible literally. He was an extremely intelligent man, acutely aware of the sensitivities he faced in his new venture both with Jews and Christians. Christianity, he pointed out, is a far more theoretical way of life than Judaism. Christians were not geared to doing things but rather to believing and to praying. They must be mobilised into acting rather than just agreeing with Israel's right to exist. Zionists they must be, if they believed in their Bible; and not only believing Zionists, but practical Zionists. The greatest Zionist of all time, proclaimed the Reyerend Van der Hoeven, was God himself; for does the Bible not tell us:

"Then he will raise a signal to the nations and gather together those driven out of Israel; he will assemble Judah's scattered people from the four corners of the earth" (Isiah 11:12)

The strongest threat to the continued existence of these Christians in Israel came not from the PLO, whom they called "the army of the Devil" but from public suspicion in Israel itself, that the Christian Embassy may be a cover for missionary activity. Many Christians believe that not only must all the Jews of the world come back to Israel but at the time of the Second Coming all the people of the world will also accept Jesus as the Son of God and become Christians. To counter this the Christian Embassy had, after two years of fumbling with contradictions, taken a clear stand on the issue of proselytising. A year previously, when I asked the Reverend Van Hoeven whether or not the Christian Embassy condoned missionary activities, I was unable to obtain a clear denial from him. Instead he had answered that we Jews must understand that spreading the word of Christ was a central, fundamental duty of every practising Christian. However, they now stated categorically and unambiguously that they were against all missionary activity **within the State of Israel**. Their sole purpose was to foster a right and proper relationship between Christians and Jews, in order to atone the guilt of and abolish forever Christian persecution of the Jews (which they openly confessed) and to aid and abet the return of the Jewish People to their God-given land. This new position, they claimed, had been revealed to them by the Lord in their dilemma which threatened to halt their holy mission altogether. The question of whether the whole world will turn Christian had mercifully been relegated to the End of Days when the Messiah will arrive.

There was much preoccupation with Messianism in Jerusalem. The preaching of many Jewish converts, like Daniel, to the Jewish people to fulfil God's commandments, in particular by obeying the rituals, is motivated on their own admission, by their concern with facilitating the coming of the Messiah.

It is ironic that now that the Jews have abandoned the original goal of the Zionist Movement, "the in-gathering of the exiles", which envisaged the return of *all* the Jews of the world to Israel, some fundamentalist Christians should have taken it up for an entirely different reason, namely, to facilitate the second coming of their Messiah.

It is also ironic that while many Jewish Messianists opposed Zionism insisting that only the Messiah can lead the Jews back to Israel, many Christian Messianists were now among the most ardent Zionists in the world, because they believed that all the Jews of the world must return to Israel before Jesus will return to Earth for the second coming. Like the Jews and Gentiles in New York, the Christian Messianists have become more "Jewish" while the Jewish Messianists have become more "Christian" in Jerusalem!

CHAPTER 18

WHOSE TEMPLE, WHOSE HOLOCAUST?

I had always taken for granted that the Hebrew Bible was ours. The Christians co-opted our Bible and renamed it the **Old** Testament. The Moslems edited it to suit themselves and for my part they were both welcome to make of it what they liked. But it was my ancestors, the Jews, who had written it and to me it was **our** Book - the mythology, history, law and ethics of the Jews.

I had never thought much about the Bible or its endless interpretations before I came to live in Israel. But there I learned about a fifteen hundred-year-old charade which the Jews had been forced to engage in, of reconciling their Biblical teachings with those of Christianity, often on pain of death. I knew instinctively that no Jew ever cared tuppence how any non-Jew chose to interpret the Jewish Bible, but I could not for the life of me understand the obsession of the Gentiles with how the Jews understood their own Bible.

Similarly, I had always assumed that the Temple Mount in Jerusalem on which we Jews had built the First and Second Temples before either Christians or Moslems existed, was none other than ours. But sometime between 685 and 691 A.D. the Moslems built themselves a splendid mosque (the Dome of the Rock) smack in the centre of the Temple Mount, because Moslems believe this to be the site mentioned in the Koran which tells the story of the miraculous night journey of Prophet Mohammed to a rock located above the exact place which in Jewish tradition had been God's original dwelling place - the Holy of Holies.

Before 1967, when the Israelis captured the Old **City** of Jerusalem, no one except religious Jews who turn twice a day from the four corners of the earth to pray facing it, ever thought about the Temple Mount. No one cared that Jews had been barred from praying there since

1948, when the Old City had been captured by the Jordanians. Few Muslims journeyed from anywhere to visit it. Since 1967, when Israeli soldiers liberated the Old City from Jordanian rule, hundreds of thousands of Jews have come from practically every land on earth to pray at the Western Wall, the only surviving remnant of the Second Temple.

I have a sneaking suspicion that if the Jews were to forget about their Book and their Temple Mount, so would everyone else. There seems to be an insatiable need to claw at the beliefs and traditions of the Jews, a sort of sibling rivalry like kids squabbling over a toy which only holds attraction for a brother or sister as long as the other wants it.

But never in my wildest imaginings could I have dreamt that the day would dawn when anyone would want to wrest the Holocaust from the Jewish People. When I first read "The Diary of Anne Frank", I had no doubt that this was the story of a Jewish girl suffering the fate of Jewish victims of the Germans' plan to liquidate the Jews. Unlike with Shakespeare's Jessica, I had

had no trouble identifying with Anne Frank. I first read her diary when I was about her age and I too was in the grip of an intensely passionate and totally ungratifiable first love for a Jewish boy who had suffered Hitler's obscenities. Unlike with Shakespeare's Shylock or Dicken's Fagin, I had had no trouble recognising my own parents in Anne's mother and father and my own uncles in Anne's uncle. They would have said and done the same things in similar circumstances.

The house below the attic where Anne had hidden was converted into a memorial museum after the war and in 1998 Yasser Arafat, the chairman of the Palestinian Liberation Organisation, made an official visit to the Anne Frank house. The Israeli government immediately criticised the visit as a publicity stunt. After expressing his heartfelt sympathy, Arafat appropriated the Anne Frank story for the Palestinian cause. The Israelis were now the Nazis and Anne was now a Palestinian child. Images of Anne wearing a Keffiyeh, the badge of Palestinian resistance, have since been used for propaganda against Israel. In 2010 Iman Aoun, the director of the

Astor Theatre in Ramallah produced a series called "The Gaza Monologues", each one based on moving stories of 31 Palestinian teenagers about Anne's age, matching the suffering of these children to the experiences of Anne during the Holocaust.

In Jerusalem the Israelis have erected a memorial, the Yad Vashem, to the six million victims of the Holocaust. It is not only a monument but also a repository of archives and documents and an institute for research into the causes and events of the catastrophe which resulted in the annihilation of over one third of the Jewish people.

In the winter of 1983, I attended a lecture in this Holocaust Museum by Professor Mommsen, a German historian, whose thesis was that the German people were unaware of what was happening in the death camps until after it was all over.

As I sat listening to Jewish historians refuting this preposterous claim, I realised that we were playing a new act in an old drama, another cycle in the never- ending debate with the inquisitors of the Jewish people.

Now I was hearing the first rewriting of the history of the Holocaust. The crucifixion of Christ had four re-drafts of the story of the crucifixion in the new Testament from Matthew, Mark and Luke to John; each one successively shifting the blame from the Romans to the Jews. The Jews have ever since been engaged in a two-thousand-year defence of themselves against the charge of the killing of Christ, finally gaining acquittal from Pope Paul V1 in 1965 not by their useless polemics but at the price of the Holocaust - six million Jews for one!

I sat there in the warm, carpeted auditorium in the Holocaust Museum not really hearing the evidence and counter-evidence being bandied to and fro on the rostrum but anticipating in my mind where Prof Mommsen's lecture was heading.

Thirteen million people died in the Nazi concentration camps of whom six million were Jews. And within one generation of its occurrence the Jews are already defending their claim to the Holocaust as they have for centuries to their Book and their Temple Mount. Just as the Christians reinterpreted and the Muslims rewrote our ancient history, others are now endeavouring to rewrite our Holocaust:

"It was a typical Jewish exaggeration" the anti-Semites claimed.

or "It didn't happen at all"

"It was a Jewish lie" the neo-Nazis said.

"It was not six million Jews that were murdered, *only* five*"* Prof Mommsen now proclaimed.

Professor Mommsen is not a neo-Nazi nor an anti-Semite. He is a good German. He was introduced in the auditorium of the lecture hall at *Yad V'shem* as a friend of the Jewish People on this, his fourth visit to Jerusalem. He is a respected and responsible historian. As a German he tells us he is concerned to discover how the murder of five (not six) million Jews could have happened in his country. The official figure he accepts is between five and six million. He consistently referred only to five throughout his address. He also refers to the Holocaust as *"this business"*. Never once in this whole lecture on Holocaust did the word Holocaust pass his lips. After establishing his "bona fides" and expertise in the matter with a welter of facts and figures, he suggests that the German people had no idea about *"this business"* until it was all over. Six million (or five - we are so blunted by the sheer magnitude of *"this business"* that a million more or less, makes little difference to this intellectual exercise), were systematically exterminated over a period of six years and the German people knew nothing!

How is it possible, I wondered, that six million people (or even five) were identified, rounded up, smoked out of hiding, transported from practically every country in Europe, sorted for immediate murder or slave labour and never heard of again and the German people managed to know nothing of "this business". The infra-structure of people required to organise transport, build concentration camps and gas chambers, guard the camps, conduct prolonged biological experiments on human guinea pigs, assign inmates to work gangs and oversee slave labour projects, organise the torture drills, collect, sort and store the belongings and incinerate the bodies of six million people (or even five), must have directly involved many thousands of Germans who physically entered and left the precincts of the camps each day.

Thousands of Germans must have actually ***witnessed*** "this business"; thousands could not have escaped the stench of burning human flesh even with their eyes closed and ears blocked. Thousands of German guards must have gone home, some daily, some on leave, to their families and friends, distributed across the length and breadth of Germany, with news and mementos: perhaps a diamond ring or a gold wedding band as a coming-home gift for a loving, lonely wife, or a child's doll still warm from its dispossessed owner in search of a new mother.

But Professor Mommsen maintained the German people knew nothing about "this business" because they had suppressed the information which their conscious minds suspected. They looked away, did not want to hear or see and did not ask. They knew that Jews were disappearing but never imagined that five (or six) million were systematically being murdered.

I started to search my own memory for evidence to rebut this new rewriting of Jewish history. I recalled reading newspaper reports that soap and lampshades were sold in German shops during the war clearly labelled as produced with human fat and human skin. I decided that I would to go to the archives tomorrow and check this out.

The next day several Israeli and a couple of American Christian historians took the floor in turn to counter Professor Mommsen's claims with further impressive arrays of documents, facts and figures. . I felt as though I was drowning in the hopelessness of Jewish impotence. For a whole semester I had sat through a course of lectures on the Holocaust at the Hebrew University which had been one monumental saga of impotence. Every effort, every scheme, every plea, every ploy to save the Jews of Europe during World War II had ended in failure. Now we were at it again, trying to save not six million people, but six million memories! The very exercise seemed obscene. Why should we forever continue to be engaged in this futile exercise of proving the truth to those intent on destroying it?

Suddenly I remembered my own first-hand evidence. My own aunt and uncle, when arrested by the Gestapo in 1942 in Paris for deportation to Germany, physically threw their twelve-year-old son out of the house, screaming at him to get away from them. I, too, had by now had twelve-year-old children of my own and I knew that there could be only one condition under which a parent would abandon a child in the midst of a war to fend for itself and that is the certain knowledge that one is going to one's death. So, by 1942 Jews in Paris already knew what awaited them in Nazi concentration camps, but according to Prof Mommsen the German guards who arrested them did not. But these German guards knew that Jewish parents tried to hide their children, never to see them again and they executed Gentiles who cooperated in this ploy. I wanted to raise my hand to speak, but I quashed the impulse. Nor did I return to the *Yad V'shem* to check my facts on soap and lamp-shades.

There should be no further discussion between us, for all discussion is futile. If some Germans think they can absolve their guilt of the Holocaust by denying knowledge of its existence or its magnitude, so be it, for now we have a *Yad V'shem* in which the evidence of the Holocaust will be preserved for future generations, as long as we have a gun with which to defend it.

The last speaker, Gideon Hausner, the Chief Prosecutor at the trial of Adolph Eichmann in Jerusalem in 1962, now took the floor. He brought no facts or figures, no dialogue or discussion to counter Professor Mommsen's thesis.

"Professor Mommsen's interpretations are based on his premise that the German people did not know that Jews were being systematically annihilated during World War II. Well, I submit to you that they did!"

That's all. Dr. Hausner sat down.

There was no point to further disputation. Two thousand years of disputation could not restore Matthew's version of the crucifixion. Only Israel can.

CHAPTER 20

WUS BIST DU? (What Are You?)

I only became aware of much that held me to this country once I came close to leaving it. My husband was unhappy in Israel. After six years I gave up hope that he would someday adjust to Israeli society and I finally agreed to leave. It was a snap decision on my part as all big decisions in my life have always been. But I knew, from long experience to trust such snap decisions because they only surface after long incubation and are usually right.

I was happy, sometimes deliriously happy, in Israel. But I could not continue to enjoy such happiness indefinitely at someone else's expense - certainly not my partner's. And so, at one of our regular discussions of

David's discontents with life in Israel, the words just slipped out quite effortlessly, because they were there ready to emerge:

"I'll go with you if that's what you really want. And what's more I promise not to bear a grudge against you and to make the best of whatever we do. But you'll have to make all the arrangements yourself. I could not actively leave but I will follow you if you go."

A weight seemed to lift off him. He straightened up, became active and involved for the first time in years. The transition appalled me. I could only conclude that what he had been protesting was really true: that he felt imprisoned, cut-off, ineffective, inarticulate, alienated and hostile in Israel. I had always assumed that this was dramatic exaggeration. I had thought he was just being flippant when on one occasion when we were disembarking at Bombay airport, he had said that he felt as though he were returning to civilization after getting out of Israel.

Now I remembered my own reaction to this country in 1952 when nothing short of prison bars could have kept me from leaving and began to understand the depth of his discontent. I felt confident in my decision that the time had come to give up trying to hold him here. I had had six years and now it was his turn. In a few short years Aviva would be finished school and we would be able to spend part of our time in Israel and part elsewhere as many people now do and I knew that David would be happy with such an arrangement even though he was now protesting that he never wanted to set foot in Israel again. I had been through this love-hate cycle myself. He was passionately involved in Israel's internal politics and her survival and this I knew would be my lifeline back to Israel from the Diaspora.

But for the moment a weight had lifted off him at the thought of leaving and had descended on me. I felt as though I were in mourning. I awoke the next day with a lump in my chest. Everything and everyone continued to function as before but my connection with them had suddenly been ruptured.

I began to visualise myself back in the Diaspora, on the outside looking in. Without really being aware I had become emotionally involved in the minutia of Israel's daily progress. On my way to the local store to buy the daily bread and milk I passed the new automatic car-wash which had been installed just yesterday in our local service station. People had come in their hundreds to witness the first car being sucked into the cleaning area by the enormous rotating iridescent blue brushes and emerge from out the other side several minutes later clean as a whistle. To us Israelis the first automatic car wash in Jerusalem was symbolic of Israel's development which filled me with pride. Tomorrow such scenes would be meaningless for me.

At the local store a macho Israeli in his early thirties jumped the line of little old ladies waiting to pay for their groceries. The day before I would have intervened. It was an accepted custom in Israel that if you had just a small quick matter to transact you could butt into a conversation or a queue of people to avoid waiting. But this was inevitably abused by little matters becoming big ones and stronger people ousting weaker ones. Once when standing in a line to buy theatre tickets I noticed after ten minutes of no progress in the line that people were quietly approaching others closer to the counter to buy tickets for them; not one or two but dozens of tickets. Little syndicates had formed, appointed a representative who approached someone, friend or stranger, to act as agent for the whole group. I was so enraged by this spectacle that I literally jumped on a soapbox which happened to be at hand on the sidewalk and in my broken Hebrew told them what I thought of this shameful behaviour. Those at the back of the queue were roused to action by my audacity and a free-for-all broke-out around the ticket office. The attendant closed the window and the line reformed with perfect Anglo-Saxon decorum.

I had been waiting to buy my tickets with a friend who had lived in Jerusalem for thirty years.

"You would not have done that if you'd had someone up front getting your ticket" he said amused at my anger.

"You're wrong you know" I replied. "It's the principle, not the tickets, that's important to me."· "Why should Israelis do things the way a small minority like you thinks right? You're living in Israel now, not prim and proper Australia. Anyway when in Rome…"

But that was just it! He'd hit the nail on the head. I was no longer in Rome. In Australia I was in Rome. Since the year dot, I had been in Rome, doing what the Romans do. Now I was in my home country, *chez-moi*. Now *we were* the Romans. Now I could do it *my way*.

"Why did you come here?" Jewish tourists from all over the world asked me repeatedly. I told them I came in search of my identity, my roots, my reality.

"And have you found your roots and your identity in Israel" they would ask. To my own amazement I thought I had.

" But" I hastened to add, "I don't *feel* like an Israeli. Here in Israel, I feel no more genuinely Israeli than I felt genuinely Australian in Australia" : in Israel, I am an Australian, in Australia I am an Israeli.

When I was very tiny my parents spoke to me in Yiddish because they knew little English at that time. I think I must have learnt to understand Yiddish before English, yet there was never any stage in my life when I spoke it. But there was one short sentence I deigned to utter, perhaps prophetically:

"*Wus bist du*" ("What are you") My parents would ask me, like some mantra.
And I would answer:
"A *Yiddishe maidele*" (a little Jewish girl.)

"*Wus bist du*?" I ask myself now.

"A *Yiddishe maidele*" is still all that I can honestly reply.

ABOUT THE AUTHOR

Born in Sydney, 1932

Melbourne University, (1952-56 and 1962- 65), BSC degrees chemistry, biochemistry, psychology, and psychopathology

Worked in the field of population control for United Nations in Singapore (1966-68), London School of Hygiene and Tropical Medicine (1969-72), Columbia University, New York (1973-75).

www.ingramcontent.com/pod-product-compliance
Lightning Source LLC
Chambersburg PA
CBHW070546160426
43199CB00014B/2395